SPIRIT OF THE
HORSE

PaRragon

Bath New York Singapore Hong Kong Cologne Delhi Melbourne

This edition published by Parragon in 2009

Parragon
Queen Street House
4 Queen Street
Bath BA1 1HE, UK

Copyright © Parragon Books Ltd 2004

Designed, produced and packaged by Stonecastle Graphics Ltd

Photography by Bob Langrish
Text by Nicola Jane Swinney
Edited by Kate Green
Designed by Sue Pressley and Paul Turner

ISBN: 978-1-4054-9848-7

Printed in China

CONTENTS

HORSES ON FILM

The horse has been a part of our lives for many centuries and to capture the fitness, power and agility of this most beautiful animal on film has been my passion for the last thirty years.

PHOTOGRAPHING THE horse at liberty, in the freedom of wide-open spaces, has often presented a challenge – from trying to get close to a group of nervous wild Mustangs by crawling (down-wind) on my hands and knees over rough terrain, to sitting patiently, coaxing a new-born foal out from behind its protective mother. But the key to success is to understand the horse's mind – the way it thinks and its strong natural instincts for survival.

Many times I have turned a stallion free in a pasture and it has only taken a few minutes to capture *the* single picture which shows him at his best; at a collected canter or an extended gallop which illustrates his strength and power, or at a floating trot where he will almost walk on air with all four hooves off the ground in a moment of suspended animation. The stallion will perform a pattern in his field, repeated many times until the initial excitement is replaced by curiosity. At this point it is possible to capture his character as he turns his attention on the photographer.

Often the photographer can attract his subject's attention by making different noises, including the sound of a 'growling bear' when the horse may be surprised and turn as if to say: 'What was that?'. This is when he is likely to be at his most expressive.

Foals and groups of youngsters are always fun to photograph because they are naturally inquisitive, and it is possible to use their curiosity to achieve the perfect picture. If you scare a group of yearlings they will run away, bunch up together and walk back to you as a herd to check you out, ears forward and eyes popping out of their heads. Foals will always hide behind their mothers, but if the photographer sits quietly in the middle of a group he will soon have some close friends and great pictures.

At all times it is prudent to be aware of the instincts of the horse when entering its territory and to respect the way it thinks or you risk frightening it away or jeopardising your own safety by failing to understand its language of signals.

Photographing horses has taken me all over the world – to every continent, from the Russian herds in the Caucasus Mountains to the wild Mustangs of America. I have captured over 190 breeds with my camera, from the tiniest miniature horses to some of the largest horses in the world, and I have been privileged to photograph many of the world's most beautiful and valuable equines.

I hope you enjoy the images in this book and that they evoke something of the nature and spirit of this most magnificent animal – the horse.

Bob Langrish

SPIRIT OF THE HORSE

Why do I love horses? Well, what's not to love – how could anyone, looking at the sumptuous photographs in this book, fail to be rendered speechless with admiration and adoration?

IT IS difficult to imagine that there might be those who fail to be moved by these beautiful, generous and intelligent creatures but indeed, my parents are among them. They couldn't understand my complete obsession with all things equine from the moment I realised that horses existed. Like many youngsters, I spent my entire childhood at the stables: grooming, mucking out, riding, or just inhaling that unmistakable sweet scent of horse. I think I probably drifted amid a miasma of 'horse' for most of my formative years.

But the horse is so much more than a pet or a mere conveyance. Countless times I have heard owners say of their horse or pony, 'he's such a nice person'. If you don't own an equine, you would probably think they were being rather precious, but those who do will be nodding sagely – to them, the horse is a *person* with a strong individual personality.

While the horse has been an integral part of our lives for centuries, it is all too easy to forget that he is, essentially, a wild animal. We radically change the lives of our horses so that they can fit into ours.

But, thankfully, there are still herds of truly wild horses and it is a joy and a privilege to see them in their natural state; to watch them frolic and play, and kick up their heels with the sheer exuberance of living.

I remember, many years ago, we had a heavy snowfall one night in April and had to rush over to the stables to bring in the mares and their foals. It was four o'clock in the morning and icy cold; we were all somewhat befuddled with sleep and spent an hour chasing the youngsters around the field. The foals thought it a huge joke and would let us get just close enough to touch them with the headcollar before wheeling off again with boundless energy; racing and prancing – and snorting loudly into the freezing air. Just horses being horses.

In this book, you will find no pictures of horses being ridden nor in harness, just this most beautiful animal as he was meant to be – a free spirit. From the tiniest foal to the largest Shire, the unparalleled glory of the horse is showcased to perfection.

Of course everyone has their favourite, and I hope, within these pages, you will find yours. Will you be seduced by the cheeky charm of a little Welsh foal or will the Arabian's beauty win you over? Will you be enchanted by the majesty of the striking Andalucian or impressed by the magnificence of the Friesian, or, like me, will you find it impossible to single out just one? I hope you enjoy this book as much as I have enjoyed writing it and that, together with the stunning images, my words will convey something of the spirit of the horse.

Nicola Jane Swinney

Chapter 1
WILD HORSES

WILD HORSES

To the true horse lover, the realisation that this magnificent creature, this half-tonne of bone and muscle, is essentially a wild animal only adds to his mystique.

W E ARE so accustomed to his domesticity – the riding school hacks, the docile ponies at summer fêtes – that to see the horse in his natural environment, whether it is the open plains of America, the Australian outback or the comparatively tame mountains and moorlands of the UK, brings us up short. We forget that he is part of our lives because of his nature, not just our coercion.

No other animal has lived so close to humans, nor captivated us for so long. From his early domestication, he has gone with us unquestioningly to war – and often perished – he became our foremost mode of transport, and is now our companion in competition and leisure. His destiny has always been linked with that of man. Yet swathes of our planet are still populated by wild horses, and how tragic it would be if that were to change. Where Darwin's law of survival of the fittest rules, the horse will continue to evolve and thrive and benefit man for years to come.

Naturally gregarious, horses are herd animals – any horse owner will know that horses turned out together in a field are likely to form a 'pecking order', or hierarchy, and will, for the most part, remain as a group, even if they are of quite different types and breeds. Likewise, in the wild, horses

Above: *A powerfully built little horse, the Przewalski's diminutive stature belies his aggressive nature and his ability to survive in a harsh environment*

Above right: *Przewalski's Horse is said to be the last of the truly wild equines and, in 2003, a small herd was released back into the wild – for years, the only existing herds were in zoos*

> '*The Przewalski is said to be the last of the truly wild horses or ponies.*'

Previous pages: *Przewalski's Horse provides the link between the 'Dawn Horse' and today's modern breeds*

instinctively form herds, usually comprising several family groups of a stallion and perhaps five or six mares and their offspring. As a herd, they will sleep, play and feed – a wild horse will graze for up to fourteen hours a day – while constantly being alert to any danger.

Although during the mating season stallions within the groups will fight for dominance over the breeding females, the herd is usually controlled by the older mares, who will keep in check any high spirits among the younger members of the herd, particularly the colts. But while domesticated stallions are generally perceived as more dominant and unpredictable than mares, the 'matriarchs' of wild herds can be equally aggressive and far from submissive.

Safety for the wild horse is aided by a combination of excellent physical and sensory attributes – explosive speed and stamina to outrun any predator, as well as superb vision and hearing to detect any threat. For survival in the wild, the horse depends on the 'fight or flight' mechanism. He has strong, protruding teeth and as a 'weapon', particularly against another horse during a fight for supremacy, these can be formidable.

From a standing start, a horse can reach a top sprint

speed of forty-five miles per hour – about seventy kilometres per hour – in three or four seconds. His large eye, set either side of the head, has almost all-round vision, and his mobile ears, which can rotate almost through three hundred and sixty degrees, act like radar.

There is safety in numbers and a predator is likely be confused by a group of animals galloping around – an embarrassment of riches, rather than several separate meals. Here again, Darwin's theory comes into play: if a predator does manage to separate an animal from the herd, it is most likely to be old and weak or sickly, leaving the strongest, fittest members to survive and thrive. The herd's social structure, in which the co-operation of the group is combined with vigilance, ensures the safety of the individual. It also allows herd members to feed, play and rest in comparative security.

Perhaps the most famous – not to say the most ancient – of the feral equines is Przewalski's Horse, or, more accurately, pony, since this rare breed stands between twelve and fourteen hands high (a hand equals four inches or 102mm). Named for Russian explorer Colonel Nikolai Mikhailovitch Przewalski, who discovered a small herd of these animals in

the Tachin Schah – the 'Mountains of the Yellow Horse' – west of the Gobi Desert, in 1879, these are said to be the last of the truly wild horses or ponies.

Also known as the Asiatic Wild Horse, he is an eerily primitive creature and, indeed, provides the link between the earliest known horses and the modern breeds. The breed differs from its domestic descendent in that it has sixty-six chromosomes instead of sixty-four. Despite his diminutive stature, he can be fierce and aggressive. A powerfully built animal, the Przewalski has had to adapt to a harsh existence in the Russian steppes and mountains of Mongolia, where poor vegetation and severe climate have honed his powers of endurance. He is believed to be migratory, moving north in the winter and returning to the south in the spring.

Charles Darwin believed that all domestic horses descended from 'a single, dun-coloured, more or less striped, primitive stock' to which the Przewalski, with his dun colouring, mealy muzzle and eye markings, dorsal stripe and 'zebra bars' on his legs, would appear to bear witness.

In the summer of 2003, eight Przewalski's Horses, including in-foal mares, were released into Kazakhstan, where the breed had been extinct for some sixty years.

Above: *The wild Mustang of the United States of America is a real 'melting pot', with little or no breed standard – they can be any colour but are all hardy, with hard feet and a tough constitution*

Left: *The Mustang is thought to have roamed North America's great plains for around seven hundred years, having been been brought over to the New World by the Spanish explorers in the seventeenth century*

EARLY MORNING, misty dawn. Across the vast plains of the American West, nothing moves. Then an eagle, soaring high above the prairie, cries and a head lifts from a herd of horses that looked, until that moment, like a shadow. Another head, and another, eyes wide and ears pricked, and then, as one, the herd wheels about and gallops off, leaving nothing but dust and echo in its wake.

Anyone who has seen a Wild West movie, an American rodeo or even those Marlborough adverts will be familiar with the Mustang. These tough little horses populate much of North America's great plains, and are thought to have done so for about seven hundred years.

The word Mustang derives from the Spanish *mestena* – 'stray' or 'ownerless' horse – and, indeed, the breed is thought to have evolved from horses brought over with Spanish explorers in the seventeenth century. Some of those horses escaped and took up residence in the wild, forming herds. They are notoriously shy and naturally fearful of people – hardly surprising given their treatment through the years. Yet like most equines, they can be tamed and are used as 'cow ponies' – their speed and agility are renowned.

Above: *The Mustang comes in all colours, the most common being sorrel – a light chestnut shade – and bay, with skewbald, piebald, palomino, black and grey also being seen*

Above right: *Early Mustangs were thought to be escaped Spanish imports who formed herds*

Horses were thought to be extinct in America for more than ten thousand years before the arrival of the Spanish conquistadors, although horse fossils discovered in the United States show that the early equine ancestors were most certainly present.

The evolution of the horse is one of the best charted and most famous in all of science – the eventual decrease in the number of toes and the gradual increase in size; the early Eohippus or 'Dawn Horse' was no bigger than a fox – and it is believed that an incredible nineteen species of equine inhabited North America fifteen million years ago.

Hunted for their meat by both man and other predators, the horse population declined to extinction in the isolated continent until the arrival of the Spanish and their steeds, who were to change equine evolution beyond recognition.

These early imports were the Spanish Andalucian (chapter 3), Sorraia from Portugal and Barbs from Morocco and, occasionally, a 'throwback' to one of these distinctive breeds still appears in the wild herds. But for the most part, the Mustang is a stocky little horse standing barely more than 14hh, although height can vary from 13hh up to 16hh. Since his arrival in America, other breeds – such as the Morgan, Friesian and Thoroughbred – have been added to the mix.

The melting pot that these wild herds have become means there is little or no breed standard; they come in all colours, all shapes and sizes, although they all possess hard feet, sound legs and a tough constitution. The most common colours are sorrel, or light chestnut, with a flaxen mane and tail, and bay, but 'paints' – skewbald or piebald – palomino and black are also seen.

'The evolution of the horse is one of the best charted and most famous in all of science.'

With no selective breeding, by the nineteenth century the typical Mustang was likely to be coffin-headed, ewe-necked, roach-backed and cow-hocked, in other words, possessing terrible conformation – hardly a romantic ideal of the wild horse!

But while he lacks the presence and power of the Andalucian or the lithe beauty of the Arabian, the Mustang is incredibly tough and hardy, with the ability to survive in the toughest terrain, and this was what saved him. At the beginning of the twentieth century, numbers of wild horses in the USA varied from an estimated one million to two million. But, hunted for their meat and culled to protect valuable grazing land for cattle, by the early 1970s there were less than twenty thousand left in the wild. 'Mustanging', capturing and transporting wild horses for profit, became big business.

Above and previous page: *America's Mustang herds are now protected by the Wild Horse and Burro Act of 1971*

Above right: *Ever watchful, the wild Mustang has, in the past, been given all too many reasons to be nervous of man*

Right and far right: *These Mustang foals, watched over by their protective mothers, will need all their toughness to survive in the harsh conditions*

The capture and slaughter methods used were often brutal – the horses were rounded up by cowboys using trucks and helicopters and any that were injured could be left to die. The horse in North America appeared to be heading for a second extinction.

Largely thanks to the efforts of one woman, Velma Johnston – delightfully nicknamed 'Wild Horse Annie' – who led a campaign of national publicity, a law was passed in 1959 to prohibit the use of aeroplanes and motorised vehicles to hunt wild horses and burros – small donkeys – on federally owned land. This was followed, to overwhelming public support, by the Wild Free-Roaming Horse and Burro Act of 1971, which designated the Mustang a protected species under the auspices of the Bureau of Land Management (BLM).

It is hard for any horse lover to imagine these wild creatures being slaughtered to be eaten. Who among us can picture a horse, any horse, and not imagine riding him – galloping him across an open field, or feeling the surge of power beneath as he bunches his muscles to clear a fence, a ditch or a stream? Romantics will have it that the Mustang is untameable, but this is not so. Far from being the mean-spirited rebel as he is oft portrayed, he is in fact quite biddable and can form strong bonds with humans.

It is thought that the Native American Indians were the first to tame the Mustang and he changed their lives. They were hunters of the mighty buffalo and, once they had mastered the art of riding the wild horses, they were no longer at a disadvantage. It could perhaps be argued that the taming of the Mustang contributed to the decrease of the buffalo population.

Above: *At one time, there were thought to be anything between one and two million Mustang, but their numbers decreased to an estimated twenty thousand left in the wild*

Left and far left: *Tough, agile and surprisingly fast, the Mustang became a valuable asset to the Native Americans and white settlers alike*

Above: *A stocky little horse, the Mustang retains many of the characteristics inherited from his Spanish forebears*

Right: *Members of a small herd drink at a watering station paid for by voluntary contributions*

WILD HORSES

To the Native Americans, the horse meant status and nobility. He was invaluable in war, he was currency and he could buy a bride – riches indeed. When a chieftain died, his horses were sacrificed to join him on the 'other side'.

But it wasn't long before the white man – the cowboys – discovered the Mustang as a means for transport rather than a substantial meal. The nimble little horse seems to possess an inherent 'cattle sense' in that he is almost able to anticipate what a cow will do next, which secured his place as the cowboy's preferred mode of transport.

Today, this skill can be seen in Western riding competitions, where the Mustang excels. He is also used in rodeo and for pleasure riding. The Mustang remains a protected species and the Bureau of Land Management still monitors the herds. It even offers an adoption scheme to ensure America's wild horses continue to thrive.

'To the Native Americans, the horse meant status and nobility. He was invaluable in war, he was currency and he could buy a bride – riches indeed.'

Left: *Although rarely standing more than 14hh, the wild ponies do bear some horse-like characteristics, hinting of their ancestry*

Above and above right: *There is little nourishment on the marshland of Assateague, off the east coast of North America, but the ponies of Assateague and Chincoteague are what is known as 'good doers'*

'Highly intelligent and versatile, the Chincoteague makes a suitable mount for children, who love his merry nature and colourful markings.'

Left: *A mare and foal display the typical skewbald markings of the wild herds, although solid colours do sometimes occur*

'BY MIDNIGHT, the swell had increased drastically and the moon was but briefly visible through the scudding clouds. The storm was whipping itself into a frenzy and waves slammed on to the decks. Barely, above the crashing water and shrieking wind, the horses could be heard screaming in terror.'

Fiction? Well, perhaps. But a popular theory for the origins of the ponies on the island of Assateague, off the east coast of America, and its neighbour Chincoteague, a picturesque Virginian resort, is that the ponies swam ashore from a shipwrecked Spanish galleon.

More prosaically, it is likely the ponies are descendants of herds turned loose by early settlers, but they are still believed to have been of Spanish stock. Whichever, wild horses are thought to have inhabited these islands for some three hundred years, eking out an existence from the marsh.

They tend to be small in stature, standing an average of 12hh, but do exhibit some horse-like characteristics. Their existence did not become widely known until the 1920s and they now fall under the protection of the Chincoteague Fire Department, which manages both islands.

There are two herds on Assateague, which is unpopulated by people. The island is low-lying, with little protection from the Atlantic storms, and much of it is sandy marshland. There is a saying that the Chincoteague pony 'can get fat on a cement slab' – in other words, he is a 'good doer'.

Highly intelligent and versatile, he makes a suitable mount for children, who love his merry nature and colourful markings – most of the ponies are skewbald and piebald, although solid colours do occur. An infusion of Arabian blood has improved the quality of the herds.

Every July, the ponies are rounded up on Assateague and swum across to Chincoteague, where they are auctioned. Those unsold are swum back to their island the following day.

Above and right: *Wild horses are thought to have inhabited the islands for three hundred years, eking out an existence from the marsh*

'A popular theory for the origins of the ponies is that they swam ashore from a shipwrecked Spanish galleon.'

Left: *It is said that this small hardy horse owes its size to the sparse vegetation available on the islands*

'The word Brumby is thought to have derived from the Aboriginal word baroomby, *meaning wild.'*

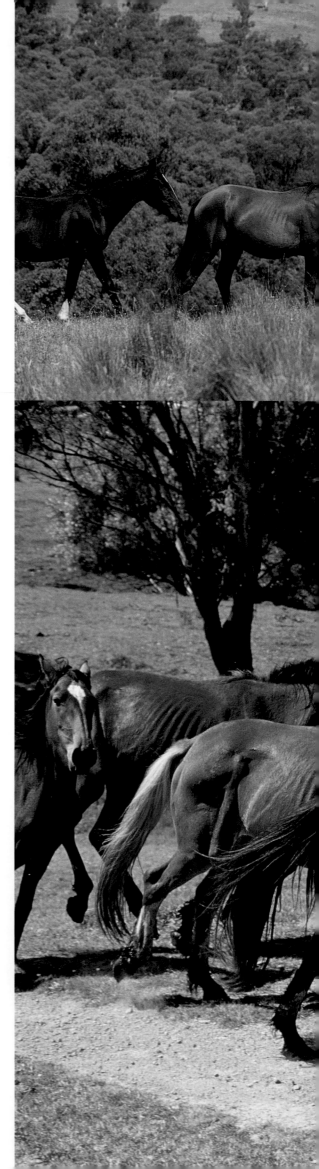

HE IS often called Australia's national icon, yet the Brumby – the continent's only feral equine – has been, of all the wild breeds, perhaps the most persecuted.

Horses arrived in Australia with First Fleet in 1788, which brought English Thoroughbreds and Spanish horses. The long journey by sea was arduous and only the toughest survived – man and beast. Later, more Thoroughbreds were imported, along with Arabians and ponies. The Brumby, much like the American Mustang, descended from these early imports.

But in Australia, he is seen as a pest species, competing with cattle for food and water. The lack of selective breeding means many Brumbies are of poor quality and they are deemed by some to be too intractable to be used as riding horses. Indeed, the word Brumby is thought to have derived from the Aboriginal word, *baroomby*, meaning wild.

Because the feral herds adapted to the terrain and climate, they were prolific breeders and spread across the vast outback. They were hunted for their meat or shot to preserve pasture, and water supplies were fenced off.

Today, estimated numbers vary between three hundred and six hundred thousand. But in the summer of 2003, a further cull was in prospect – to stop them entering the Namadgi National Park in Canberra. The environment ministry said that if Brumbies had to be destroyed to keep them out, this must be done as 'humanely' as possible.

Brumby Watch was lobbying to try to stop the cull and to preserve the feral horses of the Antipodes.

Above and right: *The Brumby is seen as a pest in Australia, competing with cattle for food and water in the harsh terrain*

Above: *The Camargue's thick white coat protects him from the cold winters and harsh winds of the region, a vast swampland in the Rhône delta*

Above right: *The wild ponies on the Camargue are known as 'the white horses of the sea' and only about thirty herds currently exist*

Left: *There is little to nourish the Camargue horses, yet the herds thrive on the region's stunted grass and reeds – they will always manage to find something on which to feed*

THEY LOOK like ghosts; all grey, moving almost silently through the marsh in the early morning mist. Only the occasional whicker or a splash as they walk through the shallow water gives away their presence. These are the wild horses of the Camargue, a vast swampland in the Rhône delta in the south of France. There is little to nourish them here, where all that grows is stunted grass and reeds and where the mistral – the notoriously cold, strong north wind – howls across the delta.

Winters in the region are harsh, but these hardy creatures – known as 'the white horses of the sea' – thrive and breed here. Their foals are born black, brown or dark grey, but they lighten with age; the older the pony, the lighter the colour.

Their thick white winter coats offer excellent protection against the freezing temperatures suffered in the Camargue region – unless they get wet in heavy snow and quickly get cold. Fortunately, this is a rare occurrence.

There are only about thirty herds – or *manades* – comprising an estimated forty-five stallions and four hundred mares. In many places across the Camargue, the horses are maintained to improve the condition of the land; without the grazing herds, the land would be covered by shrubs and brambles and would become impenetrable and fallow.

Stallions are rare because, generally, they are captured and gelded (castrated) to be used as mounts. The chosen few remain entire, selected by the ranchers on the delta to produce future stock.

For two months of each year, starting in April, the selected stallion is allowed to run with a herd, of which he is lord indeed. If two stallions meet, a fierce and violent battle is almost inevitable. The stallion will mate several times with a mare who has come into heat, often watched curiously by the rest of the herd.

A mare will usually start bearing foals from her fourth year and, all being well, will continue for the next fifteen, giving birth each spring. Slow to mature and short in stature – the Camargue rarely exceeds 14hh – they are renowned for their longevity, living well past twenty-five years.

Although they have probably been indigenous to the region since prehistoric times – they bear strong resemblance to ancient cave drawings – the Camargue was only recognised as a breed in 1968.

They possess good bone and a hearty constitution. Their thick white coat offers excellent protection against the elements and their feet are generally hard and sound. They are no beauties, though; their heads are often coarse, necks short and the whole picture rather primitive.

But what they lack in looks they make up for in performance. Their active, high-stepping action makes them much prized by French cowboys – the *gardians* – who use them to drive the fierce black bulls of the area.

Now that some seventeen thousand acres of the Camargue is designated a national reserve, the white horse of the sea has a niche in the tourist industry – forming an integral part of this romantic landscape.

Right: *The horses of the Camargue actually help to maintain the land – without the grazing herds keeping the vegetation in check, vast areas would become impenetrable and the land would lie fallow*

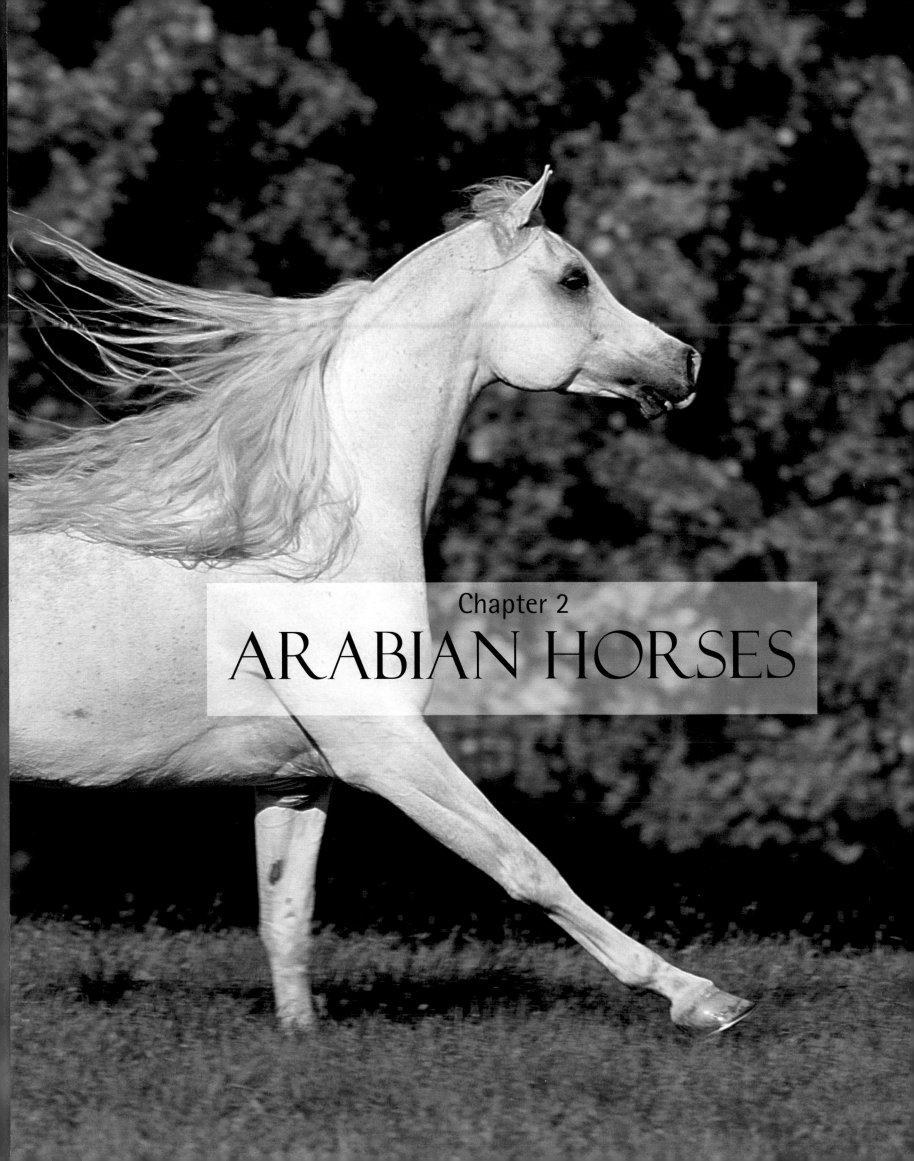

Chapter 2
ARABIAN HORSES

the Arabian's huge, wide-set eyes, upwards to a point between the ears and down across the top third of the nasal bone.

His elegant neck sweeps gracefully to a rounded wither and strong, sloping shoulder, while his short back, with its high croup, is notably concave. He has a broad, deep chest encasing exceptionally strong lungs, which give the breed an ability to work unfailingly for considerable periods of time and make them ideal for endurance riding. Added to this are clean, hard legs – they are deceptively delicate, but Arabian bone is said to be denser than that of other breeds – and good, sound feet, which are almost perfect in shape.

Indeed, as much as he is prized for his beauty, the Arabian is revered for his speed and stamina, as well as his athleticism. His action is a joy to behold – he moves freely and lightly, as though on springs – as he appears to float. The long, silky mane and tail, which is carried exceptionally high, all contribute to the horse's enchanting appearance.

The Arabian is not a big horse, rarely exceeding about 15 hands high. The grey colour – which, as with all breeds, lightens with age – adds to his fairy-tale charm, but all solid colours, except palomino, are seen. His coat is fine and silky, so the veining can be seen beneath, and has a high sheen, particularly in the chestnut and bright bay.

This beautiful ancient breed is thought to go as far back as 3000BC and has strongly influenced many of today's more modern breeds of horse.

Above: *It is easy to see the* jibbah, *the shield-shaped bulge between the wide-set eyes, on this typical grey Arabian*

Above left: *This stunning chestnut Arabian stallion has an almost metallic sheen on his fine and silky coat*

Previous pages: *This Arabian stallion epitomises the fairy-tale quality of this unique and beautiful breed*

'His action is a joy to behold – he moves freely and lightly, as though on springs – as he appears to float.'

It is said that when Allah created the horse, he said: 'I call you Horse; I make you Arabian and I give you the chestnut colour of the ant. I have hung happiness from your forelock which hangs between your eyes; you shall be the Lord of the other animals. Men will follow you wherever you go; you shall be as good for pursuit as for flight; riches shall be on your back and fortune shall come through your mediation.' Then Allah put on the horse the mark of glory and happiness – a white star in the middle of the forehead.

In proclaiming that Allah had created the Arabian, the Prophet Mohammed believed that those who treated the horse well would be rewarded in the afterlife. This, coupled with the belief that 'no evil spirit will dare to enter a tent where there is a pure-bred horse', encouraged further

breeding of the Arabian. As time went on, the Bedouin tribes of the Arabian deserts zealously protected and maintained the Arabian breed, striving to keep it *Asil* – or pure – in the form intended by Allah. Any mixture of foreign blood from the mountains or the cities surrounding the desert was strictly forbidden.

The Bedouins' highly selective breeding policies shaped the magnificent horse we see today, and who – through centuries of care and commitment – remains highly prized.

Because of the harsh desert conditions, the Arabian would work alongside and share food and water – and even, sometimes, accommodation – with his nomadic masters and, as a result, he developed a close affinity with man and high intelligence.

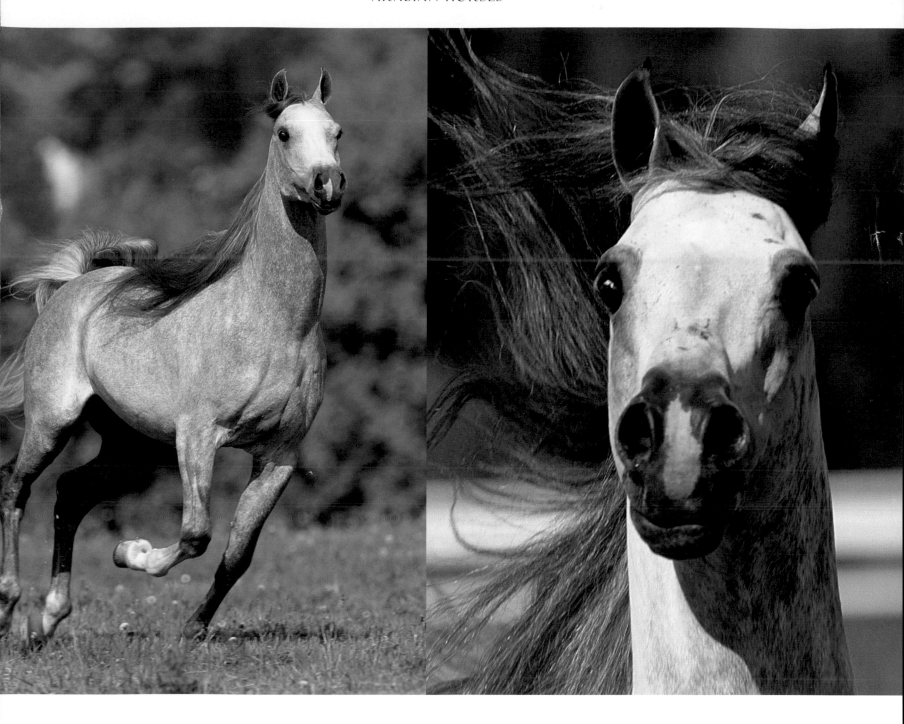

Much prized, the Arabian was primarily an instrument of war. A well-mounted Bedouin could storm an enemy settlement and capture the tribe's herds of camels, goats and sheep, adding to his own tribe's wealth and, subsequently, to its status. Such a raid was extremely risky, and could only be achieved by taking advantage of both surprise and speed of the attack – and making good the escape.

The Arabian mare was deemed best for such forays, as she would not whicker to the enemy's horses, warning the tribe of the attackers' approach. These wonderful war mares exhibited great courage in battle, taking charges and spear attacks and giving no quarter. Speed and endurance – for which the Arabian is still famous today – were vital, as the raids were often carried out far from the tribe's own camp.

Above: *Note how far this Arabian's eyes are set apart, and his flaring nostrils*

Above left: *This Arabian illustrates the tiny, curved ears, dished or concave face, large liquid eye and small muzzle that typify the breed*

Far left: *This magnificent horse was bred by the Imperial Egyptian Stud in the USA – Egyptian lines remain highly prized, both in the US and in Europe*

The Arabian mare was thus beyond price. Mare families, or strains, were named according to the tribe or sheikh that bred them. Hence the five basic families of the breed were Kehilan, Seglawi, Abeyan, Hamdani and Hadban. Although all combine the beauty and athleticism we associate with the Arabian, to the aficionado they are easily identifiable.

In all these major strains, the most common colours were grey, chestnut and brown or bay. Black was not a popular colour, as it absorbs heat and a desert horse would not be as efficient with a black coat. Diligent breeders did their best to eliminate the colour from their prized bloodlines. However, today most Arabians no longer live in the desert and black horses are becoming increasingly popular.

But each of these five distinct strains, when bred pure, developed recognisable characteristics, which made them readily identifiable. The Kehilan strain was noted for depth of chest, masculine power and size – the average height for Arabians of this strain was 15hh. Their heads were notably short and had an especially broad forehead, with exceptionally wide jawline.

Above: *All solid colours are permissible in the Arabian, apart from palomino, but black, like these mares, bred in California, is still relatively uncommon, although it is becoming more popular*

'The five basic families of the breed all combined the beauty and athleticism we associate with the Arabian.'

Right: *This magnificent black stallion, bred in the UK, displays the legendary 'mark of happiness and glory' – a white star – clearly on his forehead*

50

'The Bedouins' highly selective breeding policies shaped the magnificent horse we see today, and who remains highly prized.'

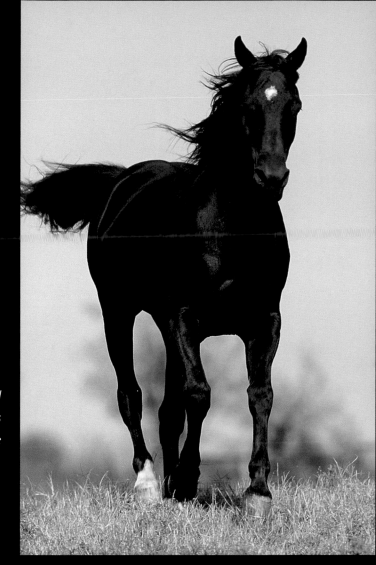

Left: *Highly intelligent, the Arabian is alert to his surroundings*

Right: *Showing the spirit associated with the breed, this fine horse is clearly enjoying life*

Below: *Fast and agile, with a wiry athleticism, this mare lets off steam – note her beautiful flowing tail*

The Seglawi Arabian was particularly refined, possessing almost feminine grace and elegance. He had fine bone and stood only about 14.2hh, with a longer face and neck than the Kehilan. This sleek little horse, although perhaps lacking in stamina compared with his larger brothers, was renowned for his speed.

Similar to the Seglawi, the Abeyan strain was also refined, and pure-breds had longer backs than a typical Arabian. Like the beautiful Arabians shown here, the Seglawi was most commonly grey, with more white markings than other strains.

In contrast, the Hamdani horse could be considered plain – if that description could ever apply to the Arabian – with an athletic build and bigger bones. He lacked the pronounced *jibbah* and had a straighter profile and neck. He was a bigger model, standing at about 15.2hh.

The Hadban was a smaller version, standing under 15hh. Although he had a markedly muscular build and bigger bone, he was known for his gentle and tractable nature. The primary colour was brown or bay, with very few, if any, white markings.

Substrains developed in each main strain, named after a celebrated mare or sheikh. But all had one thing in common

Top and above: *The Arabian's action is second to none – he appears to float, as if on invisible springs*

Left: *Although a roan colour at present, this foal may well turn grey like his mother. Note her distinctive high tail carriage, a defining characteristic of the Arabian breed*

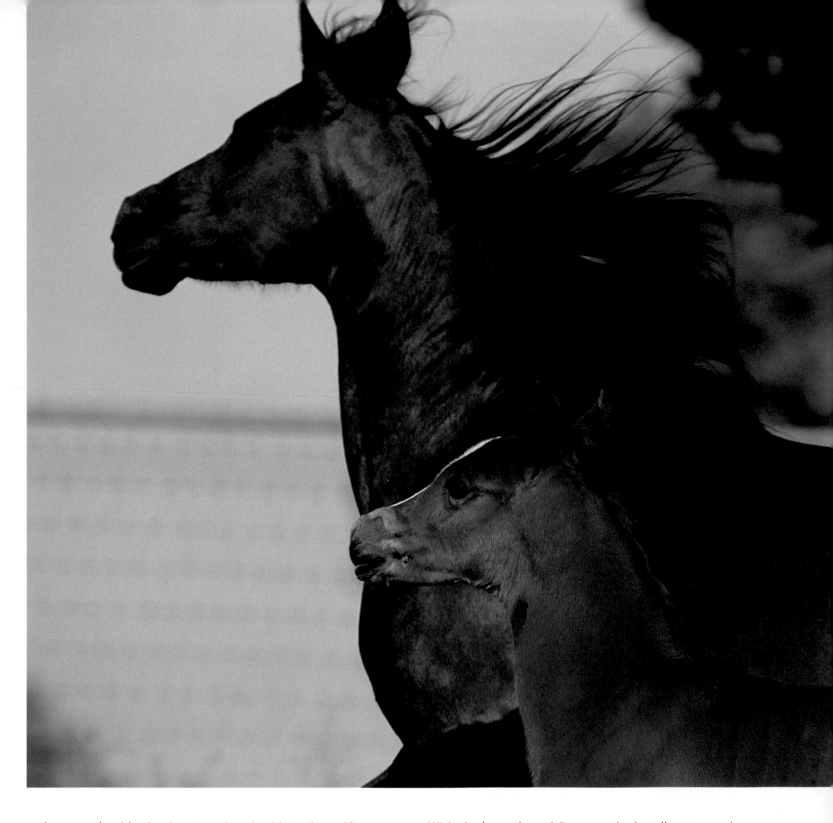

– they were bred in the desert, and evolved into the swift, graceful and powerful mount of the Arab warrior. Possessing both speed and stamina, these remarkable horses were coveted by all who saw them and these superb steeds influenced the breeding of horses around the world.

It would be almost impossible to overestimate quite how influential these early Arabian horses were on the development of modern breeds. Horses were bred in Europe to carry a knight and his armour and lighter equines owed a lot to the pony breeds. The Europeans had nothing to compare with the swift, sleek horses of the Arab invaders. Rumours of the 'Eastern' horse spread, with ever more fantastic tales of their speed, stamina and athleticism.

With the invention of firearms, the heavily armoured knight became defunct, as did his weight-bearing charger; now cavalry was clamouring for lighter, faster and more nimble horses. Increasingly, wars proved the superiority of the Arabian and he became the mount of choice for the world's military. But it wasn't just the military who desired the horse of Arabia. To own such a horse carried increasing prestige, for this marvellous creature would improve local stock beyond measure. The Arabian became almost invaluable – Europeans of means, predominantly royalty, would go to almost any lengths to procure one.

A revolution was to take place in the history of horse breeding. For the Arabian – although regarded with scorn by some factions of the modern horse world – played an enormous role in the development of the highly prized English Thoroughbred.

Three imported stallions formed the foundation of the Thoroughbred: The Byerley Turk, imported in 1683, The Darley Arabian in 1703 and The Godolphin Arabian in 1730. Ninety-three per cent of all modern Thoroughbreds can be traced back to one of these three bloodlines on the male side.

The Byerley Turk was owned by Colonel Robert Byerley, who was thought to have captured him from a Turkish soldier in Budapest in the 1680s. Famously, the colonel took the horse – said to be a 'particularly substantial Arabian' – to the Battle of the Boyne, where he escaped capture thanks to his steed's fleetness of foot.

Above: 'What are you looking at?' Curious, alert and intelligent, this baby is secure at his mother's side and shows no fear

Above left: Mirror image – how similar are this mare and her foal, pictured at an Arabian stud in California; they both show the same proud head carriage

'The Arabian mare was beyond price and mare families, or strains, were named according to the tribe or sheikh that bred them.'

Left: *This lovely mare shows the fluid action of the breed, while her enchanting chestnut foal has a pronounced dished face*

'The Arabian played an enormous role in the development of today's highly prized English Thoroughbred.'

Left: *The beauty of the Arabian is unsurpassed and he was to become almost invaluable in improving existing stock*

Right: *The Arabian possesses speed, strength, stamina and soundness, all of which benefited the Thoroughbred*

Above: *This Arabian stallion has all the spirit and fire found in the breed, which also has an exceptionally gentle and tractable nature*

Left: *Arabian mares turned out at an American stud come to see what is going on – their interest and curiosity are an indication of the high intelligence possessed by the breed*

The Byerley Turk was retired to stud around 1690, standing first at Middleridge Grange in County Durham and then at Goldsborough in Yorkshire. The horse is said to have stood at stud for some eleven years, so he obviously possessed stamina as well as speed.

Also standing at stud in the north of England, The Darley Arabian sired perhaps the greatest racehorse of all time, Flying Childers, who was unbeaten in all his eighteen races. The Darley Arabian was acquired by Thomas Darley, British consul in what was then Syria, and was described as 'a horse of exquisite beauty'. He stood at the Yorkshire stud belonging to Darley's brother. Little is known about the third stallion, The Godolphin Arabian, although he is thought to have been born in the Yemen and brought to England by Edward Coke of Derbyshire. Edward Coke, a renowned livestock breeder of the day, discovered the stallion as a five-year-old pulling a coal cart through the streets of Paris, although this may be apocryphal. Coke later sold him to Lord Godolphin.

But the influence of the Arabian does not stop at the English Thoroughbred. His bloodlines enriched and enhanced such diverse breeds as the Welsh Mountain pony, whose dished face and neat muzzle are reminiscent of more exotic ancestry; the Austrian Haflinger and his Italian counterpart, the Avelignese, trace back to the Arabian stallion, El Bedavi, and the Orlov Trotter, an eighteenth century carriage horse developed in Russia, originated from an Arabian cross. The Lipizzaner's exclusive grey colour is owed to Arabian blood, while the Morgan horse of America is thought to have been of predominantly Arabian and Thoroughbred ancestry.

Indeed, the part the Arabian has played in the development and refinement of other horse breeds throughout the world is unmatched.

It has been said of the Arabian: 'It is the oldest bloodstock of all; it is a tap root, not a derivation from anything else at all. It has the gift, possessed alone by true root stock, of absolute dominance in breeding and unrivalled power of impressing its own character on any other breed with irresistible force. The Arabian is the chief and noblest origin of our national racehorse, of the best breeds of North Africa, and of light horses all over the world.'

Today, there are still distinct Arabian strains and types. Perhaps the most famous line is that of the Crabbet Stud, founded in Britain before the turn of the nineteenth century by Lady Anne and Sir Wilfred Scawen Blunt, who bought horses from the desert Bedouins and imported them from

Above: *This glowing creature illustrates the striking characteristics of her breed*

Right: *A perfect demonstration of the 'floating action' with tail held high*

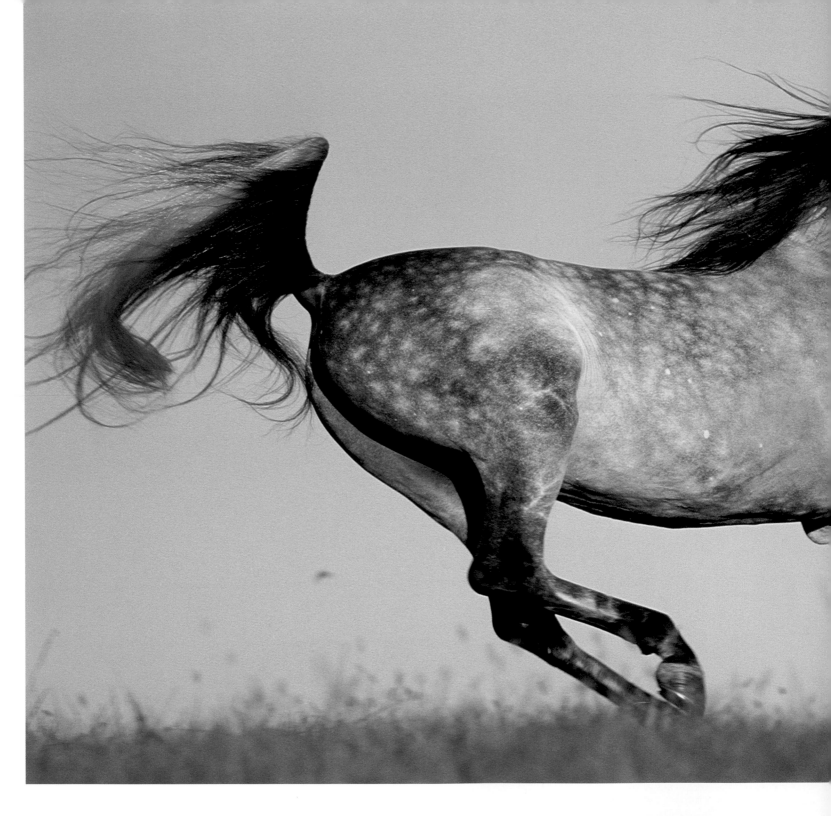

1878 onwards. One of the most important was a mare, Rodania, and the stallions Mahruss II and Mesaoud. Crabbet lines, though increasingly rare, are highly valued and the description can only be applied to Arabians descended from lines owned by the Blunts.

The Egyptian Arabian, too, is greatly prized, being descended from the herds of Mohammed Ali Pasha and his grandson Abbas Pasha, as well as twenty horses from Crabbet sent to Lady Blunt's Sheikh Obeyd Stud in Egypt. President Nasser of Egypt subsequently gave a stallion, Aswan, to the Tersk Stud in Russia, where he was widely used on racing lines and mares of Polish breeding. Polish Arabs are known for their substance and beauty.

The Persian Arabian – though similar to his better-known counterpart – is thought to be older by some fifteen hundred years, although numbers are now greatly reduced. Very much alike in characteristics and conformation, he is slightly stockier but possesses great presence and bearing.

In Hungary, the Shagya Arab was developed in the eighteenth century. The country's oldest stud, Mezőhegyes, was founded in 1785, but the Babolna Stud, founded in 1789, is now famous for its Arabian horses. The Shagya is a practical horse with more bone than the Arabian, and is predominantly grey in colour, although he is named after a cream stallion on which the breed was founded. The stallion was big for an Arabian, standing just over 15.2hh, and gave

Following pages: *The Arabian horse has had an almost unquantifiable influence on the world's modern breeds*

Left: *This fine stallion was bred at the Imperial Egyptian Stud*

Below: *The pure-bred Arabian will continue to be revered for his great beauty*

the Shagya breed its substance. In France the emphasis is on racing and so French Arabians have been bred to resemble the Thoroughbred more closely than their English counterparts. Australia has also produced some superb Arabians, whose strong limbs and hard feet allow them to excel at endurance riding.

The USA is a comparatively young nation in terms of horse culture, but it has the distinction of having the largest population of pure-bred Arabians in the world. Throughout the world, the Arabian horse has made his mark. Revered for his purity, diligent breeding keeps those exalted bloodlines undiluted. And his enduring beauty means he will be in demand for centuries to come.

'The part the Arabian has played in the development and refinement of other horse breeds throughout the world is unmatched.'

Chapter 3
IBERIAN HORSES

IBERIAN HORSES

Iberia's 'noble kings', the Andalucian and Lusitano,
are horses of great beauty, prized for their flamboyant
high-stepping action. In terms of equine development,
the horses of Spain are second only to the Arabian.

CLINGING TO the edge of the hillside, the white village glows against the cobalt sky, the afternoon sunshine glinting off the turquoise water in backyard swimming pools. An air of barely contained excitement hangs over the little town, as mothers thread their daughters' hair with flowers and flamenco music leaps and cavorts from every square.

Hooves clattering on the cobbles, the muscular grey stallions toss their heads and bunch their powerful quarters, already infected with the exuberance of the growing crowd. Their long, rippling manes and tails are decorated with brightly coloured ribbons and their arched necks are garlanded with flowers. These are the horses of Andalucia, the southern region of the Spanish mainland, and as much a part of the area's famous festival as the rhythmic snap of castanets and seductive strumming of the guitar. These Iberian kings are proud indeed; their history is long and noble and their influence on equine development, both ancient and modern, almost impossible to quantify.

Cave drawings found close to what is now Malaga on Spain's modern Costa del Sol, which date back to about 5000BC, depict a close approximation to the Spanish horse of today. In terms of equine evolution, the Andalucian – and, by association, his Portuguese cousin, the Lusitano (pictured right) – plays a major role, close on the heels of the Arabian (chapter 2) and what is thought to be his direct ancestor, the Barb. Indeed, it has been mooted that the Andalucian developed from Przewalski's Horse – or Asiatic Wild Horse – (chapter 1), or from the ancient steppe horse that is believed to have roamed the region from the Atlas Mountains and Spanish sierras to Turkmenistan. But most would agree that these horses trace back at least to the Moorish occupation of Spain in the eighth century, when the conquering invaders mixed the indigenous equines with their Barb horses. The Andalucian and Lusitano are but two names for these magnificent horses, which may also be referred to variously as Carthusian, Alter-Real, Peninsular or Zapatero. In order to avoid more confusion, they are perhaps best summed up as the Pura Raza Española – the pure-bred Spanish horse – or the Iberian horse.

The pure-bred Spanish horse was unified as a breed in the sixteenth century – between 1567 and 1593 – by King Philip II of Spain, who formally established the standards for the breed which is recognised today. The Andalucian name comes from the sun-drenched region of southern Spain encompassing Seville, Jerez, Cordoba and Granada, but for centuries the term Andalus referred to the entire peninsula. But the pure-bred Spanish horse still owes much to modern Andalucia, for it was thanks to an order of Carthusian monks that the breed remains pure to this day. Founded in 1476 at Jerez de la Frontera, near the coast, the Monastery of Cartuja kept a small herd of Spanish horses and preserved only the purest strains. The hot and dry climate of this area played its part in developing a breed with the hard, sound feet and fine body hair that are his defining characteristics.

Renowned as an outstanding cavalry horse from the time of the ancient Greeks – whence the renowned general Xenophon, historian and philosopher, first established the art of horsemanship as we now know it – they were prized for their flamboyant high-stepping gait and extreme agility. Fearless and beautiful, these were the warhorses of kings.

Writing in the sixteenth century, Salomon de la Broue (1530-1610), riding master for King Henry IV, opined: 'I class the true Spanish horse as the greatest. . . the most handsome, the most noble, the bravest and most worthy of kings.'

Left and above: *Beautiful and fearless, the Andalucian was prized as a warhorse*

Previous page: *A handsome Lusitano stallion has all the breed's nobility*

Above: *Approximately eighty per cent of all Andalucians are grey*

Yet the breed description does little to convey the Spanish horse's beauty and tremendous presence. The Andalucians pictured on these pages are the typical grey of the breed, although bay, roan and black are also seen. It is said that, of the modern Andalucian, some eighty per cent are grey, fifteen per cent bay and five per cent black, although these are general estimates.

He stands about 15.2hh and is compact and short-coupled, with a sloping croup (hindquarters) and low-set tail. He is known to be intelligent and his noble profile is convex – rather than concave like that of the Arabian – and rather hawk-like, with a broad forehead. His classically beautiful head is instantly identifiable. History can be read deep in his large oval eyes, set inside a triangular orbital arch and the

'I class the true Spanish horse as the greatest…the most handsome, the most noble, the bravest and most worthy of kings.'

flare of his inverted, comma-shaped nostrils hint at the strength needed for extended effort. The shape and dexterity of his upper lip are pronounced; his mouth is highly sensitive and mobile. He has a muscular, crested neck that sweeps into a long, sloping shoulder and his deep body is balanced by powerful rounded quarters. His spectacular mane and tail are typically luxuriant and often wavy. His clean legs have plenty of bone and his action is nothing less than spectacular. It is this proud action that sealed the future of the Iberian horse and for which he is famed.

It is said that when King Philip II unified the pure-bred Spanish horse, he did so to bring to life the universally idealised equine that figured so large in historical pictorials, in sculpture and in art. He selected from the basic horses bred at the time in Spain those which came closest to this ideal and instructed that only these idealised horses should be used for his breeding programme.

Horses of recognisably Spanish origins are still seen depicted in equestrian art and echoed in important sculpture – the mounted statue of King Charles I in London's Trafalgar Square is a prime example. Long coveted as the horse of the military – the Andalucian is said to be as brave and biddable as he is pleasing to the eye – with the invention of firearms in the fifteen century, the agile Spanish pure-bred was even further in demand.

The horse has a notably high degree of flexion in his hindlegs, which means he moves naturally in collection – and this agility remains highly prized and has played a part in the Spanish pure-bred's influence on other breeds.

As well as being bred as a warhorse, the Iberian breed was developed for working the lithe black bulls destined for the Spanish bull-ring and he is still used to fight in Spain's traditional arenas to this day. He is not built for galloping, but is incredibly supple and quick on his feet. He can turn on the proverbial sixpence yet, for all his fiery presence, he is gentle and docile. It is this inherently and uniformly sensible temperament that is invaluable to the *rejoneadores* – the mounted bull-fighters – who use exclusively the pure Spanish horse. While the bull-fight, which is perhaps abhorrent to some, is the domain of the Spanish, their spectacular horses are greatly prized worldwide. Although their distinctive high-stepping action – known as the gait *paso de andatura* – can work against them in the dressage arena, their athleticism is particularly suited to the movements of high school, or the *Haute École*.

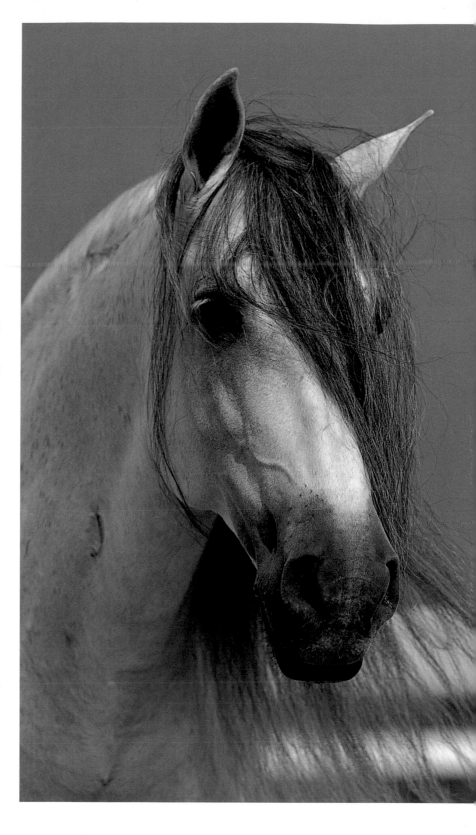

Above: *The Andalucian has a muscular, crested neck with a spectacular mane and tail which are typically luxuriant*

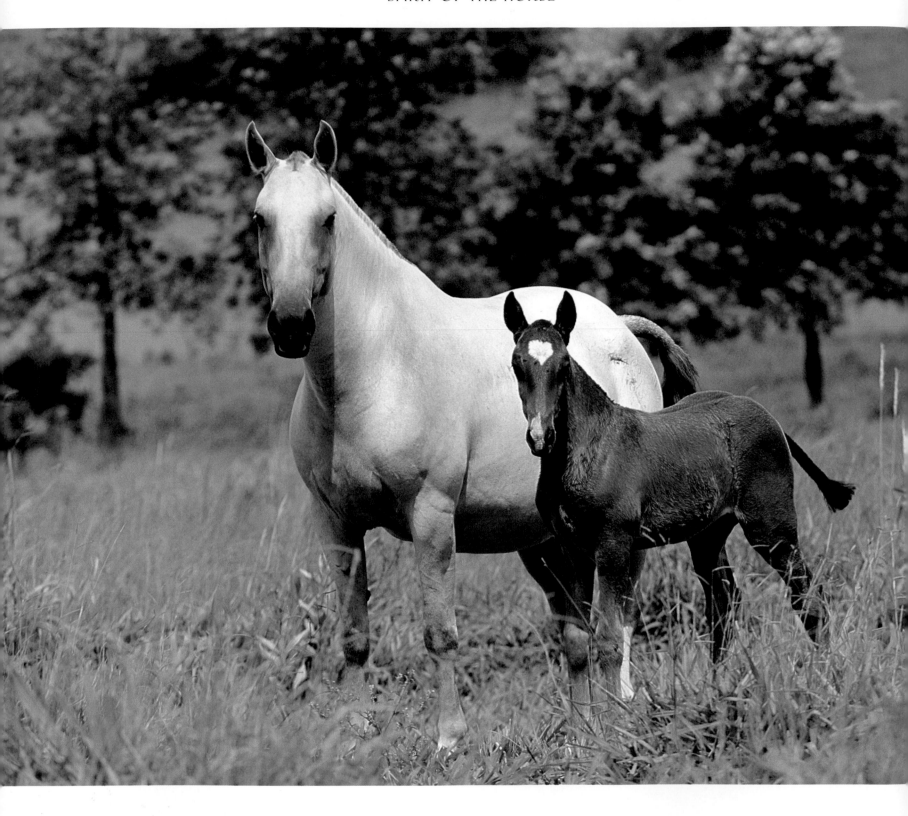

Add the Lusitano – like this mare and her foal (above) – to the mix of the Pura Raza Española and the picture gets even more confusing. Compare the Lusitano above with the Andalucian and her foal (right), and there appears little to choose between them. The Lusitano is called after the old name for Portugal, Lusitania, and although he undoubtedly has an Andalucian base, he has developed a little differently.

At a maximum of 16hh, he stands a little taller than his Spanish cousin and is what is called more 'on the leg' – that is, there is more daylight between his body and the ground.

Above: *A Lusitano mare and foal; the name comes from the old term for Portugal, Lusitania*

Right: *An Andalucian mare and foal, which stand slightly smaller than their Portuguese cousins*

Previous pages: *Lusitano youngstock*

The Lusitano, like the Andalucian, is thought to date back to a more primitive ancestor, the Sorraia, a pony that was probably a descendant of the Asiatic Wild Horse (chapter 1) and the Tarpan, which it closely resembles. There remains considerable confusion about the Tarpan – the name literally translates as 'wild horse' – an Eastern European breed, but he is generally considered to be closer genetically to the modern horse than the Asiatic Wild Horse.

The Sorraia, and the closely related Garrano of Portugal, has contributed directly to the evolution of the Spanish horse. This primitive Iberian breed was influenced by North African stock, due to the land bridge that joined Spain to the 'Dark Continent' before the last Ice Age, thousands upon thousands of years ago. The dun colour occasionally thrown up in the Lusitano possibly traces back to the little Sorraia.

The pony breed, whose name – comparatively recently coined – derives from the Rivers Sor and Raia, which run through both Spain and Portugal, still exists today. Like many breeds, he has benefited from an out-cross to Arabian blood and is now very much a miniature Iberian horse, a scaled down version of the Andalucian or the Lusitano. The modern Sorraia rarely exceeds 13hh and has a large head with the typically primitive convex profile. He is an incredibly tough and hardy pony, able to resist extremes of temperature and to thrive on sparse forage.

It could be argued that the Lusitano – whose name is also relatively new, having only been in usage since 1966 – is even more 'pure' than the Andalucian, whose infusion of Arabian blood can be seen in his more oriental head. That is not to say the Lusitano, with his large, kind eye and neat, curving ears, is not as good-looking a horse as his Spanish cousin. His pronounced Roman nose and wide forehead is set on a short, thick neck upon powerful and quite upright shoulders. He has a broad chest, with plenty of heart room; a short, compact back with well-sprung ribs, muscular quarters and long, strong legs. And, typical in the pure-bred Spanish horse, he possesses the same abundant, rippling mane and tail as the Andalucian.

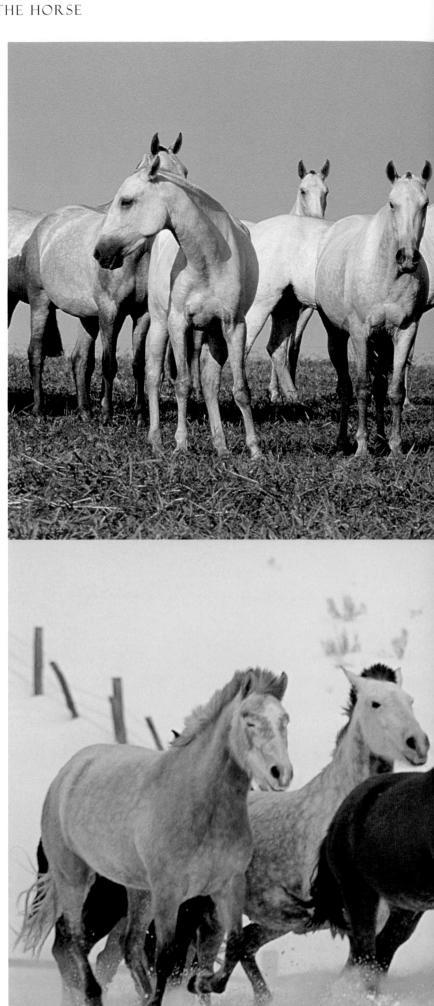

Above right: *This herd of Lusitano mares are content and relaxed in their summer meadow*

Right: *In their shaggier winter coats, this happy herd of Lusitanos appear almost stocky, almost ponyish*

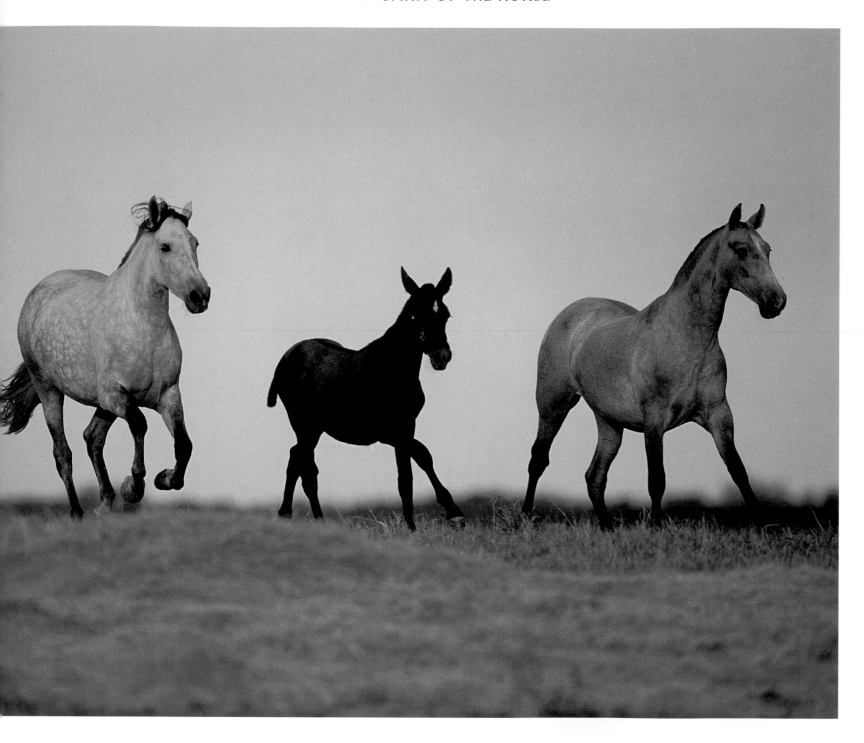

The Lusitano perhaps lacks some of the natural presence of the Andalucian, but is just as athletic and hence was equally prized as a cavalry horse and as a bull-fighter. One thing he certainly doesn't lack is speed and his elevated action and natural athleticism come into their own in the Portuguese bull-ring.

The Portuguese bull-fight is conducted entirely on horseback, so the horses must be highly schooled to swerve in an instant. It is considered a great disgrace for the *rejoneadores* if a horse is injured during the fight.

Imagine the courage it takes to face down an enraged and charging bull. As any event rider will agree, a faint-hearted horse is a dangerous horse. The Lusitano is renowned for his courage and is intelligent and responsive, traits that make him suited to the *Haute École*.

As can be seen from these three Lusitanos (above), again like the Spanish equivalent, the horses' colour, although predominantly grey, can also be black, bay or chestnut. Dun is also – though rarely – seen, as is a striking mulberry shade.

It is thought the Lusitano was developed from the Andalucian by using more Arab blood, although – as can also been seen in the grey pictured above – there is little evidence of this in the horse's tail carriage, which is noticeably lower than that of the Andalucian, and his croup is usually more sloped. As illustrated above, the convexity of the head is more pronounced in the Lusitano.

Above: *Lusitano yearlings display the wider range of colours in the breed*

Above left: *The Lusitano tends to be more solidly built than the Andalucian*

Both the Lusitano and the Andalucian are becoming increasingly popular in America. The Spanish horse is thought to have first arrived in the States in the cargo holds of the conquistadors, beginning with the second voyage of Christopher Columbus.

The breed made its second official appearance in the USA as late as the 1960s, but although the importation process was slow and costly, the horses of Spain found a vast fan-base in the States, where their beauty is revered. Their elasticity makes them highly adaptable and they are used for Western pleasure and trail riding, as well as the Olympic disciplines such as dressage – at which they excel – and show jumping.

'The perfect bond between Iberian man and horse may have provided the original inspiration behind the legend of the centaurs.'

Right: *The Andalucian is said to be as brave and as biddable as he is pleasing to the eye.*

'A horse of enormous presence, he was in great demand as a cavalry mount.'

Below: *This impressive Andalucian stallion is a fine example of his breed*

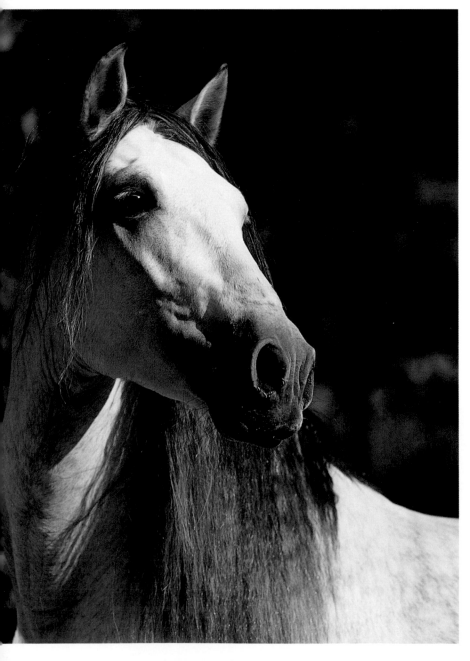

It is easy to see why the Andalucian is so in demand; the horses on these pages – all pictured in Texas, USA – show beautifully the energetic and elastic paces for which the breed is renowned. An active horse of enormous presence, he was in great demand as a cavalry mount, before his strength and courage were found to be invaluable in the bull-ring and on the farms where the bulls are worked. The Andalucian is also used in a discipline that is distinctly Spanish, called the *doma vaquera*, a formalised show ring version of farm work, most closely related to a reining pattern with combined dressage elements.

However, the Spanish horse almost became a victim of his own success. He was seen as a 'specialist's mount' and, as riding became less of an academic endeavour and more of a popular sport in the nineteenth century, classical equitation declined and, with it, the Andalucian. He became almost a horse of folklore. In his book *Cavalo Lusitano o Filho do Vento*, Arsénio Raposo Cordeiro wrote: 'The perfect bond between Iberian man and horse may have provided the original inspiration behind the legend of the centaurs, a hybrid man-horse creature deemed to spring from the valleys of the Tagus River.'

Soon, it was only the great traditional families who continued to keep the Andalucian. But among these families was the Domecq dynasty – one of the great sherry producers of the region – which owned some 38,000 acres of land in the area. And in 1972, Don Alvara Domecq, the first *rejoneador* of Spain, founded the Royal Andalucian School of Equestrian Art, which was to gain worldwide renown. Situated in the heart of Jerez, the Royal School has seating for up to sixteen hundred spectators who flock every week to see the famous equestrian ballet, *Como Bailan Los Caballos Andaluces* – or 'How Andalucian Horses Dance'.

The academy is famed for equestrian excellence and trains riders of high standing, many of whom excel in more traditional dressage, such as Rafael Soto, who was seventh in the 1996 Atlanta Olympics, and Ignacio Rambla, while several of their horses have featured in medal-winning teams including at the 2002 World Equestrian Games in Jerez.

Above: *The energetic paces of the pure-bred Spanish horse make him ideal for the movements of the high school*

'The Spanish horse's strength and agility, his nobility and grace, his power and his beauty, make him a perfect dancer.'

Left: *The classically beautiful head of the Lusitano*

Portugal, too, has its own School of Equestrian Art, which uses mostly the Alter-Real, a classical high school horse that has benefited from infusions of Andalucian blood. The Spanish horse's strength and agility, his nobility and grace, his power and his beauty, make him a perfect 'dancer' and his influence stretches to those most famed of 'balletic' horses, the dancing white stallions of Vienna.

Lipizzaners (chapter 4), which are used exclusively by the world-famous Spanish Riding School of Vienna, like many horse breeds in Europe and the Americas, descend directly from the Andalucian. Spanish horses taken to Lipica – or Lipizza – in 1583 were the foundation of the Lipizzaner breed and the name of the school pays homage still to its 'Spanish' roots. It is the Spanish breed's versatility and biddability that contributed to the Lipizzaner's ability to dance. And anyone who has been lucky enough to visit the Spanish Riding School of Vienna will have seen how those wonderful white stallions really do dance.

Left and far left: *The Andalucian's luxuriant mane and tail are typically wavy*

'Spanish horses were to become the foundation stock of the many and varied equine breeds of today.'

Below: *The Andalucian has a classically beautiful head which is instantly identifiable*

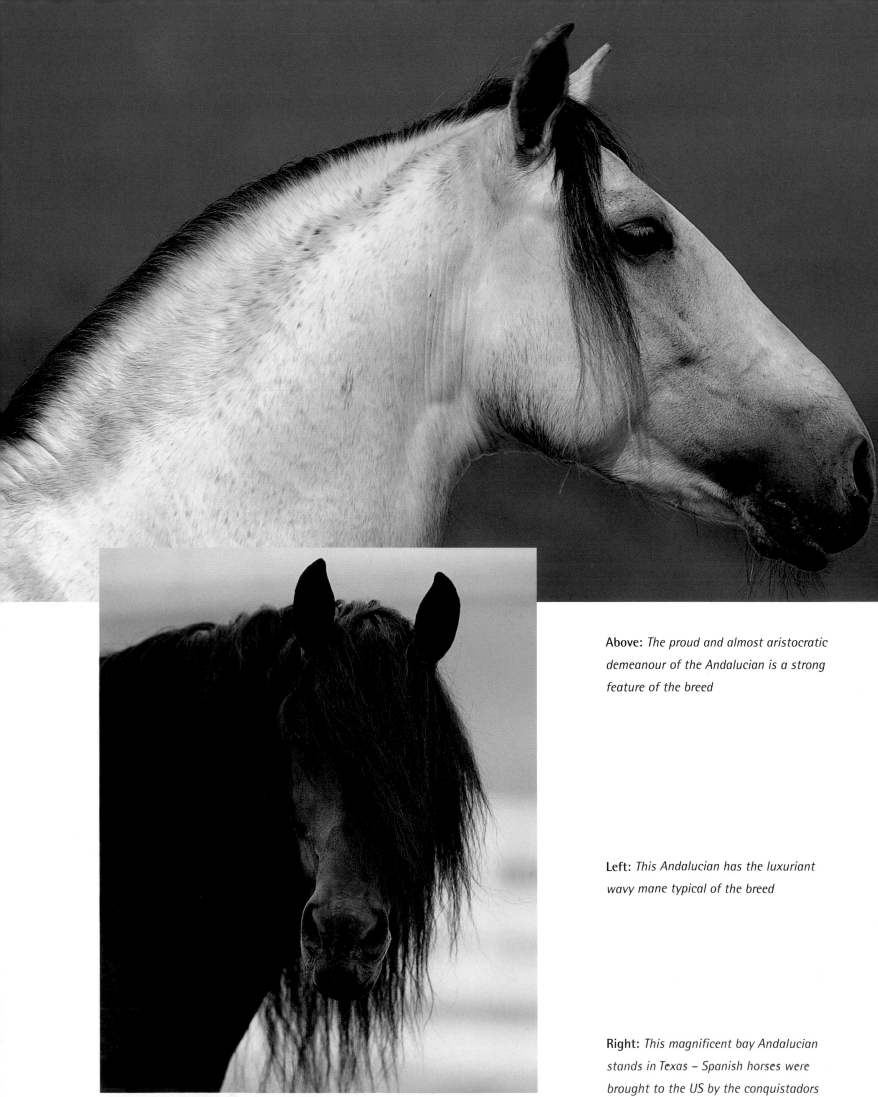

Above: *The proud and almost aristocratic demeanour of the Andalucian is a strong feature of the breed*

Left: *This Andalucian has the luxuriant wavy mane typical of the breed*

Right: *This magnificent bay Andalucian stands in Texas – Spanish horses were brought to the US by the conquistadors*

With so much history resting on his shoulders, it is fitting that the Iberian horse has such aristocratic bearing, exquisitely portrayed by this splendid Lusitano stallion (below), whose proud heritage is written all over him. And he and his Spanish counterpart (right) have, between them, played an almost unquantifiable part in the evolution of the world's horse and pony breeds.

During the sixteenth and seventeenth centuries, Andalucians were transported by Christopher Columbus and the conquistadors to the New World, the Americas, where horses had been extinct for thousands of years. These Spanish imports were to become the foundation stock of the many and varied equine breeds that today flourish across the USA – the Mustang, Criollo, Paso Fino and the distinctive spotted Appaloosa.

Right: *Andalucians like this stallion have played a major role in the evolution of the world's horse and pony breeds*

Below: *This Lusitano stallion has all the breed's beauty and nobility*

The American Quarter Horse, too, a compact and speedy little equine, is thought to have descended from Spanish horses crossed with English stallions. He is notably agile – being used for working cattle and Western pleasure riding – which he perhaps owes to his Spanish forebears. Great Britain's own celebrated native ponies, including the Irish Connemara and the Welsh Cob, and the Cleveland Bay horse which is noted for his excellent bone, all owe much to Spanish blood.

The Friesian horse of the northern Netherlands is almost an Iberian 'in negative' – here is the Andalucian's noble head; compact, strong body; sloping quarters and sturdy legs; long, rippling mane and tail, but the Friesian is always black. Spanish stock also contributed to the Kladruber, when Emperor Maximilian II founded a stud at Kladruby in Bohemia – which was to become part of the Czech Rebublic – in 1572. This magnificent horse is an Andalucian on a much larger scale; predominantly grey, he originally stood at around 18hh, but has since become smaller and more active.

The little-known Frederiksborg and his striking spotted cousin, the Knabstrup, have Spanish ancestry, too – the former being named for King Frederik II of Denmark who founded the Royal Frederiksborg Stud in 1562. The Frederiksborg was developed as a charger for the Danish military that could also be used in the riding school, in parades and in court ceremonies.

He was an elegant and spirited horse, usually chestnut, with a showy, high-stepping action. But for all this he had a tranquil and agreeable temperament, like his Spanish ancestors. The Knabstrup dates from the Napoleonic wars, during which Spanish soldiers were stationed in Denmark. They brought with them spotted horses, which were often evident in early Spanish stock.

These ancient Iberian breeds have such history and lineage that they have featured in many ancient writings. Homer refers to them in the *Iliad* around 1100BC and Xenophon had nothing but praise for 'the gifted Iberian horses and horsemen'.

A horse named Babieca was the mount of Spain's 'national hero' Ruy Diaz – immortalised on the silver screen as *El Cid* – for more than twenty years. Babieca died at the age of forty and was buried at the monastry of San Pedro de Cardena, where a memorial stands in his honour.

These proud horses are rare – it is thought that there are as few as five thousand breeding Lusitano mares worldwide and there are thought to be only about twelve thousand five hundred Andalucians left in Spain today. But their beauty and presence ensure those revered bloodlines will be guarded jealously and cherished for years to come.

Above: *The beauty and presence of the Iberian horse are undeniable*

Right: *Many of the world's most popular horse and pony breeds owe some of their characteristics to Spanish foundation stock*

Chapter 4
HORSES OF EUROPE

HORSES OF EUROPE

*The demise of the cavalry mount and the rise
of the competition, or leisure, horse has led to
the refinement of European horses, who now
dominate the Olympic disciplines.*

IF YOU look at almost any European horse breed, it is likely, somewhere, that you will find at least a trace of the Arabian (chapter 2). There is no greater an example of this than the English Thoroughbred who – revered throughout the world for his turn of foot, his stamina and his beauty – is directly descended from the Arabian.

This racing machine, this eleven hundred pounds (five hundred kilos) of bone and muscle, can sprint at speeds of more than forty-five miles (seventy-two kilometres) per hour and can jump a distance, lengthwise, of some thirty feet (nine metres). He is bred to race and will race like the wind,

using all his might to be the one who gets his head first past the post. But he is not just glorying in his fantastic power; his yearning and determination to be first is bred into him, an echo of his herding history and 'fight or flight' instinct. First is strongest, mightiest and best. First is supreme.

Of all the world's breeds, the Thoroughbred is the fastest and the most valuable, and on his back rests a multi-billion pound racing and breeding industry. The racecourses of Britain, the USA, Japan, Australia, New Zealand and France echo with the resonating thunder of his hoofbeats and the names of exceptional horses reverberate down through the

Previous pages, below and right: *The Thoroughbred may be any solid colour, except palomino, with white markings, although the most common colours are variations of brown, chestnut and bay. Grey Thoroughbreds owe their colour to their Arabian forebears*

'Ninety-three per cent of all modern Thoroughbreds can be traced back to three foundation sires.'

centuries. Britain has a long history of 'running horses', and there were already several racecourses in existence before King James I set up the race track at Newmarket in the seventeenth century.

It is said that Richard the Lionheart devised the first race – for which he donated three prizes – on Epsom Moor. The native stock of running horses was probably created by mixing Spanish, Neopolitan and Barb blood with the Irish Hobby – an antecedent of the Connemara pony – and the Scottish Galloway, as well as other native breeds. But, as throughout history, man wanted better, faster, stronger, and so the monarchy and nobility who were the participants in racing sought to find a breed designed primarily for speed.

There was a vital element missing in these early racehorses – Arabian blood. With the introduction of the three foundation stallions, The Byerley Turk, The Darley Arabian and The Godolphin Arabian, in the late eighteenth century, the English Thoroughbred was born. Indeed, the name Thoroughbred is a literal translation of the word *kehilan*, meaning pure-bred.

The Darley Arabian sired Flying Childers, who in turn sired superb stock. His great-great-nephew, Eclipse, was perhaps the most famous racehorse of all time. He was unbeaten in all eighteen of his races and went on to sire an estimated three hundred winners. Diomed was exported to America where he went on to sire a dynasty, and the American Stud Book was first published in 1873.

With these three foundation sires – and something like ninety-three per cent of all modern Thoroughbreds can trace back to one of them – came the beginning of the fantastic speed merchant we know today. Flying Childers, Herod, Eclipse, Diomed – who won the first ever Derby in 1780 – and Matchem, and more lately, Mill Reef, Arkle and Sadler's Wells, ensured that England had the world's finest horses. The three original new bloodlines brought beauty and refinement and an enduring trait in the modern Thoroughbred – courage.

Today's racehorse is a horse of great beauty and presence, which he owes to his Arabian inheritance. Standing on average 16hh, he has a fine, lean head with a straight profile – unlike his concave-faced ancestors – with big, expressive eyes and large nostrils.

Thoroughbreds are raced at two years old, by which time their limbs may not be fully developed, but their long legs are clean and powerful, producing the racehorse's glorious sweeping stride.

First records of the English Thoroughbred were published in 1791, entitled *An Introduction to a General Stud Book*, with volume one of the *General Stud Book* following in 1808. The existence of this first 'introduction' was due to one James Weatherby, who painstakingly researched pedigree lines, and Weatherbys continues to keep records of Thoroughbred racehorses today. A horse can only race in Britain if he is registered with Weatherbys, and he can only be registered with Weatherbys if he is a Thoroughbred. His name can only be registered if it contains eighteen characters – including spaces and any punctuation – or less, and is not offensive in any way, although this last criterion has been occasionally and memorably breached.

Early Thoroughbreds were probably smaller than today's racehorses, although they were bigger than the pony racers who were competed over four miles. By now called

Thoroughbreds, the horse was bred to be bigger and faster over shorter distances – breeders wanted quicker returns on their investments, so races were shortened and the weights used to 'handicap' the runners reduced. Because the Thoroughbred no longer had to be kept hardy enough to race over the four-mile track, they could be kept inside and fed, producing bigger horses that matured earlier. Thus the stock grew finer and taller – between the eighteenth and nineteenth centuries the Thoroughbred became one and a half hands (six inches) taller – and more recognisable as our modern racehorse. Indeed, he has changed little since the mid-nineteenth century, although strains vary according to speciality. For example, the sprinter, who races over short distances, tends to be tall and leggy, while the stayer is more compact and muscled. A combination of these two types makes the classic middle-distance horse.

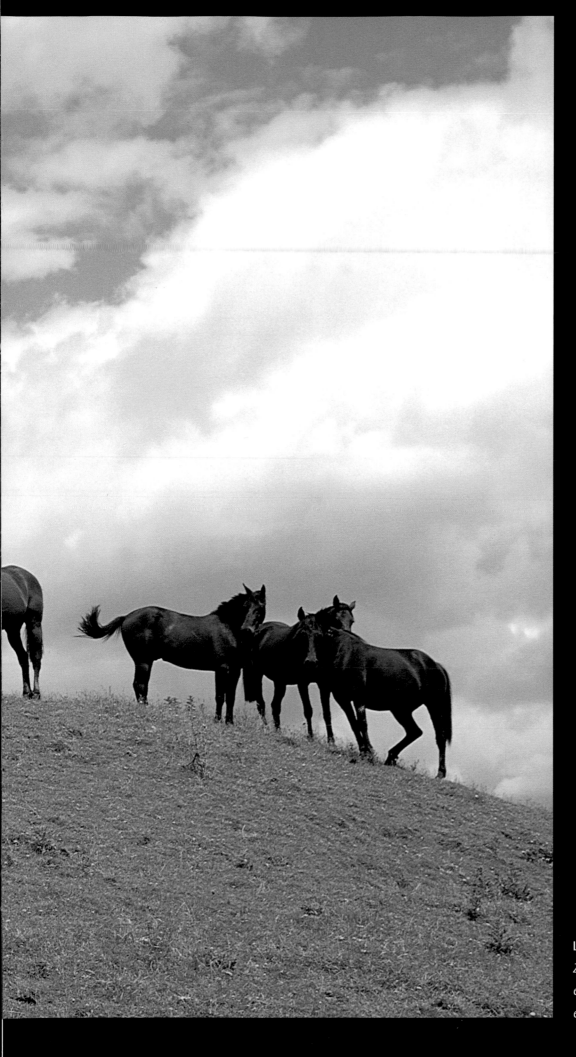

*'Today's racehorse is
a horse of great beauty
and presence, which he
owes to his Arabian
inheritance.'*

Left: *Pictured at Matahura in New
Zealand, these retired racehorses
enjoy an idyllic existence at the
end of their careers on the track*

THE FRIESIAN breed owes much to the Andalucian of Spain (chapter 3). A cold blooded horse – as opposed to the 'hot blooded' Thoroughbred or Arabian – he is a stocky draught horse based on the primitive Forest Horse of Europe. He was acknowledged by the Romans as being a superlative work horse. The breed takes its name from the Friesland region of The Netherlands and is thought to date back as far as 1000BC. Over the years, the breed did improve, as did its fortunes. The stocky horse, as well as being tough and hardy, had a sweet and biddable nature and made an excellent harness horse. He was also highly valued as a knight's charger. Although not a big horse, he had tremendous bearing and an impressive high-stepping action. During the Spanish occupation of The Netherlands in the Eighty Years War (1568-1648), the infusion of Spanish blood gave the breed more refinement.

In the nineteenth century, the Friesian – who was also widely worked as both a harness and saddle horse – was used extensively in the trotting races that were popular at the time and, as a consequence, faster and lighter specimens found favour. This was almost the end of the original Friesian, but, fortunately, a breeding plan was put into place to save the lines. Today's Friesian is a compact, beguiling little horse with spectacular paces and an endearing temperament. He stands at 15hh and has short, strong legs with hard feet and a well-muscled body. His long head has nobility and his expressive eye indicates his cheerful willingness. His neck is highly arched and he carries himself proudly. His extravagant, rippling mane and tail are reminiscent of those of the Andalucian and Lusitano. He is exclusively black, with no white markings, and Britain's Fell and Dales ponies (chapter 6) are thought to owe much to the Friesian, as does our own heavy breed, the Shire (chapter 8).

The Friesian has played a part in the development of other breeds, too, notably the Orlov Trotter of Russia; the Norfolk Trotter – a forebear of today's Hackney horse and pony – in England, and America's Morgan horse (chapter 5). Because of his black colour and superb bearing, he is popular as a funeral horse, harnessed to the hearse and decked with black plumes. He has also found a niche in the circus and early Friesians were used in the riding schools of France and Spain, where they excelled at the movements of the *Haute École*. He is still in demand as a carriage horse, where his uniform black colour makes him easy to match in a team – for competition or just for his enduring beauty.

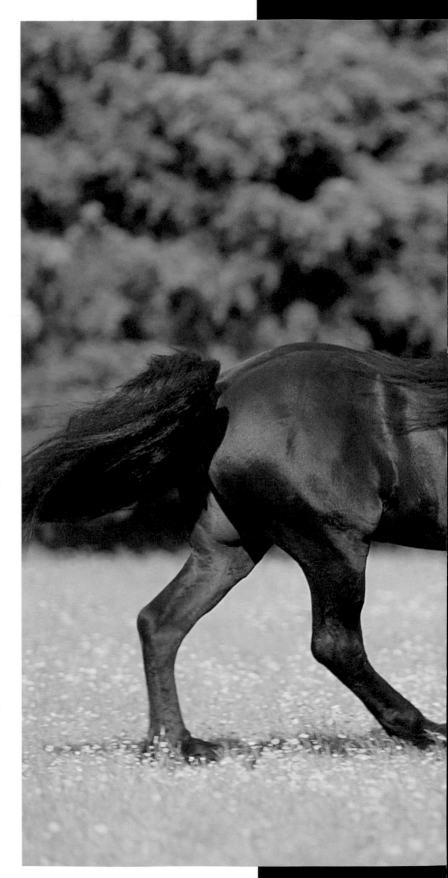

Above and right: *The magnificent Friesian owes much to the Andalucian, whose influence can clearly be seen in his noble head and extravagant action*

114

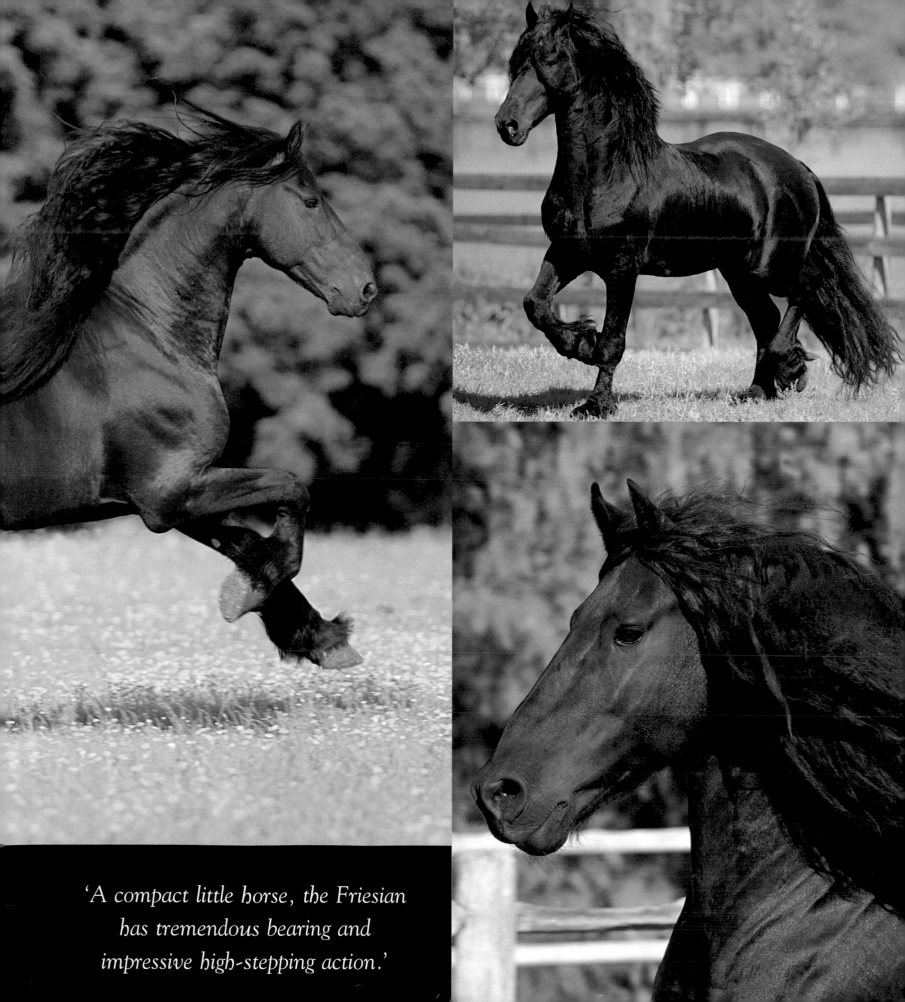

'A compact little horse, the Friesian
has tremendous bearing and
impressive high-stepping action.'

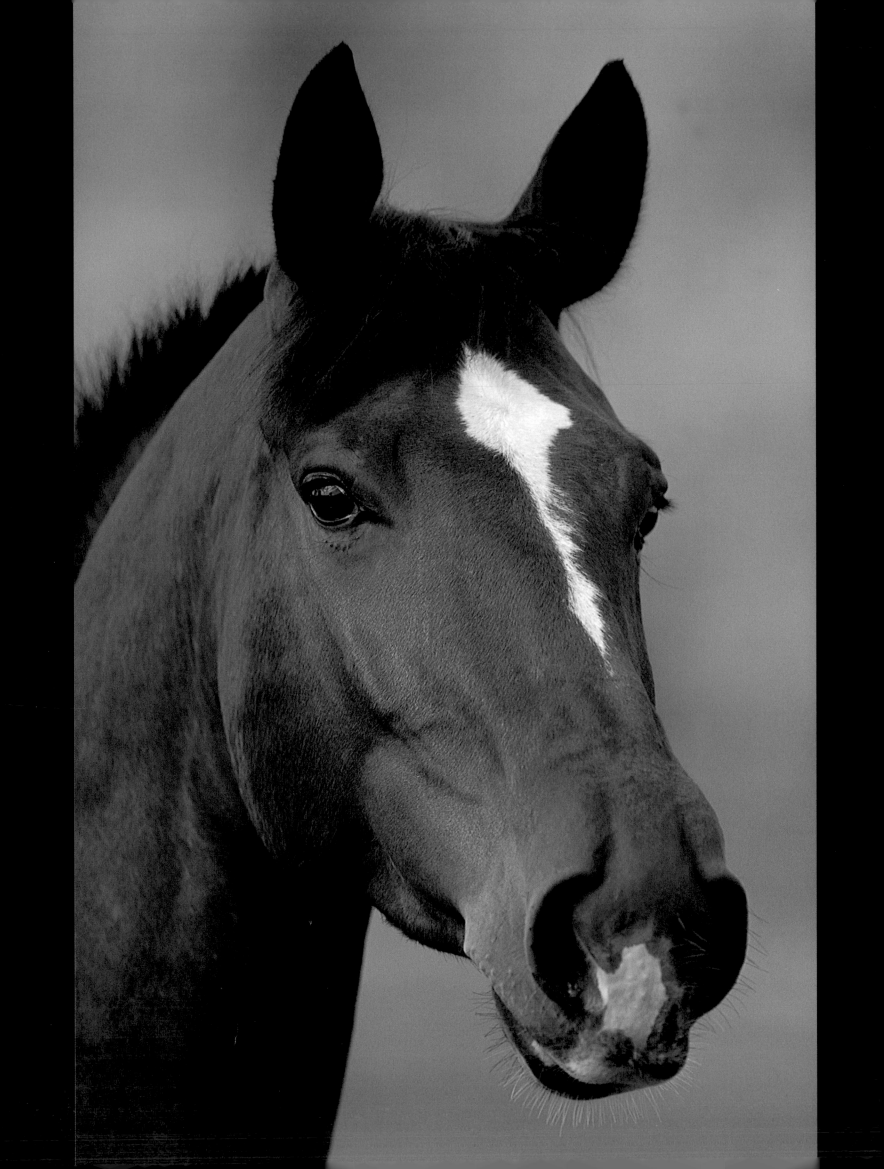

Left: *Warmbloods combine elastic paces with an amenable temperament and traditional good looks*

'The warmblood is in great demand as a competition horse and virtually dominates the dressage arena.'

Below: *The Oldenburger is the heaviest of all the German Warmbloods, which include Hanoverian, Trakehner and Holstein*

AS A success story, there is little to beat the warmblood. In the twenty-first century, he is in great demand as a competition horse and virtually dominates the dressage arena. The development of the warmblood began when breeders aimed to produce a horse that could be worked on the land, and used as a carriage horse or cavalry mount. As armaments became less heavy and cumbersome, a lighter, nimbler horse was required, and, eventually, there came the demand for a sleeker riding type, as equestrianism became less of a necessity and more of a recreational sport.

The modern warmblood is so-called because he derives from a mix of 'hotblood' – such as Arabian or Thoroughbred – with 'coldblood', the draught type based on the primitive Forest Horse. The result is a large, correct riding horse, combining elastic paces with good looks and an amenable temperament. Principal warmblood breeds include the Oldenburger – the heaviest of the German Warmbloods, as seen on these pages - Hanoverian, Trakehner, Holstein, Dutch, Danish and Swedish Warmbloods and the Selle Français.

PERHAPS THE most successful of all warmbloods is the Hanoverian, who has excelled in both show jumping and dressage, and is in great demand as a competition horse. He is a handsome creature, with powerful limbs and a long, energetic stride.

The first Hanoverians were bred at Celle, a stud founded in 1735 by George II, Elector of Hanover and King of England. The foundation stallions were Holsteins, powerful coach horses, then Thoroughbred blood was introduced to refine the stock. The Thoroughbred influence can be seen in the Hanoverian head, which is clean cut with a large, intelligent eye. Hanoverians continue to be bred at Celle, where Thoroughbreds and Trakehners are still used to develop the stock further, and where the horses are routinely performance tested to ensure they live up to the Hanoverian ideal. Emphasis is placed on reliability, performance and temperament.

Previous pages: *The handsome Selle Français, or French Saddle Horse, is a versatile and popular warmblood*

Below, right and next pages: *The imposing Hanoverian is perhaps the most successful of all the warmblood breeds*

Above: *Originally a cavalry mount, the modern Holstein is in demand as a competition horse and hunter*

Left: *The use of oriental and Spanish blood, together with a strong Thoroughbred influence, has added quality to the Holstein*

THOROUGHBRED BLOOD has also played a part in refining the Holstein, who has, over the years, been developed from a cavalry mount to a scopey competition horse, much in demand as a hunter, show jumper, eventer and dressage horse. The modern Holstein, pictured on these pages, is much lighter than earlier examples of the breed, with a finer head and generally more quality.

There is evidence of Holstein types existing as far back as 1285 in the Schleswig-Holstein region from which he takes his name. Like many of the warmblood types, he benefited from the use of Spanish and oriental blood as well as Thoroughbred, which added quality to his superb temperament.

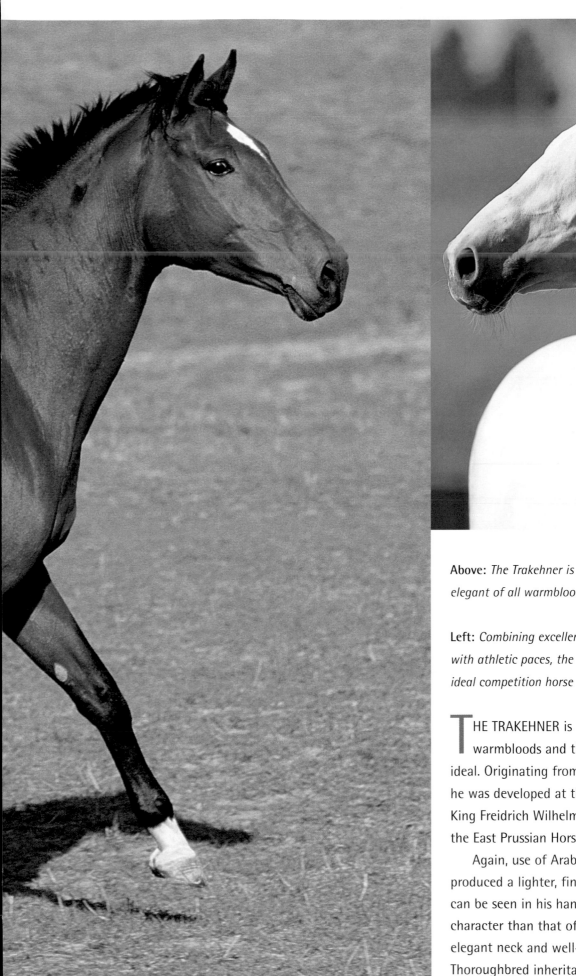

Above: *The Trakehner is perhaps the most elegant of all warmbloods*

Left: *Combining excellent conformation with athletic paces, the Trakehner is the ideal competition horse*

THE TRAKEHNER is perhaps the most elegant of all warmbloods and the closest to the competition horse ideal. Originating from East Prussia – now part of Lithuania – he was developed at the Royal Trakehner Stud founded by King Freidrich Wilhelm I in 1732 and was formerly known as the East Prussian Horse.

Again, use of Arabian and Thoroughbred blood has produced a lighter, finer stamp and the influence of the latter can be seen in his handsome head, which some say has more character than that of other warmblood types. His long, elegant neck and well-shaped shoulders echo his Thoroughbred inheritance. He stands between 16-16.2hh and has excellent, well-balanced conformation, combined with athletic, free paces and stamina.

THE SIGHT of the 'dancing white stallions' of the Spanish Riding School of Vienna is unforgettable – the magnificent horses leap and pirouette in the extraordinary 'airs above the ground' with unimaginable athleticism and grace.

These are the world-famous Lipizzaners, derived largely from the Iberian horse (chapter 3) – acknowledged by the 'Spanish' in the riding school's title – who take their name from where they were first bred in 1580, Lipizza (or Lipica), in what was then part of the Austro-Hungarian Empire.

A compact, muscular horse, the Lipizzaner is almost always grey, lightening to white, although bays are sometimes seen and one is always resident at the Vienna school. The school Lipizzaners are bred at Piber in Austria, but studs in Hungary, the Czech Republic and Romania also specialise in the breed. The modern Lipizzaner is based on just five stallions, who have their own distinct characteristics.

Above and left: *The world-famous Lipizzaner is a compact, muscular horse derived from the Iberian breeds*

SPANISH BLOOD appears, too, in the lineage of Britain's Cleveland Bay, a pack horse dating back to the Middle Ages. Formerly known as the Chapman Horse, he is one of Britain's oldest breeds.

Originally bred in the Cleveland Hills of Yorkshire, he worked the land and was used to transport huge loads of wool, on which much of the country's economy rested in the seventeenth century. He was then refined to meet demand for the taller, lighter carriage horse and is still used by England's royal courts today as a coach horse. He possesses excellent bone and substance, which he passes on when bred with other stock, and makes an outstanding riding horse.

He is also a good jumper, another characteristic which he is known to breed on and, when crossed with Thoroughbred blood, he makes a fine hunter. True to his name, the Cleveland Bay is always bay, with black points, and no white markings other than the occasional small white star.

Above and right: *In 2003, the Cleveland Bay was listed as 'critical' by the Rare Breeds Survival Trust, which monitors numbers of Britain's indigenous equines. In a survey undertaken in 1997, there were just one hundred and fifty breeding females left in Britain*

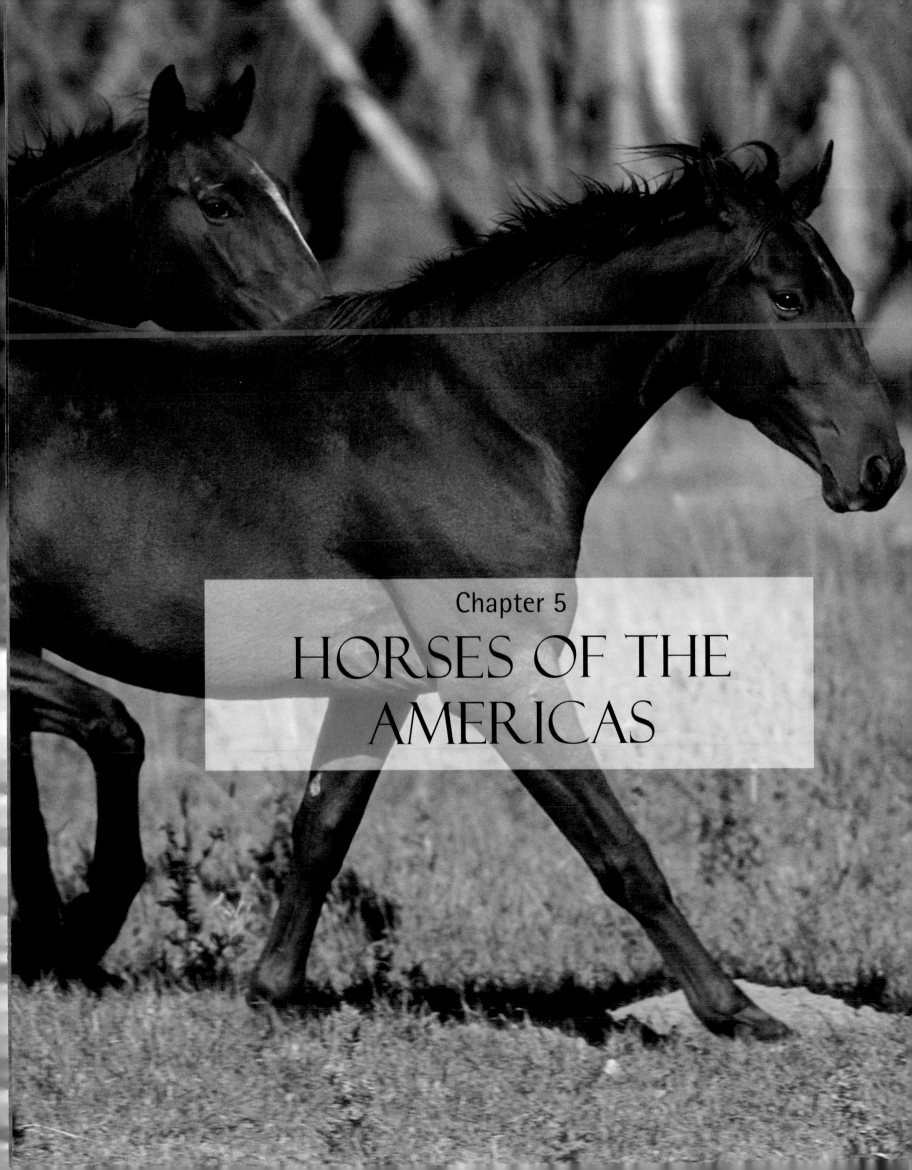

Chapter 5

HORSES OF THE AMERICAS

Above: *Turned out in the lush pastures of Maryland, this Quarter Horse certainly looks capable of 'turning on a dime'*

Above right: *This stunning pair show the typical compact and neat conformation of the breed, which is renowned for its agility*

Left: *The Quarter Horse can be any solid colour, including grey, although the most common is chestnut*

The Quarter Horse was certainly bred for speed, though, and is still the fastest equine sprinter. He is comparatively small, standing little over 15hh. He has heavily muscled quarters and hindlegs – which give him his characteristic bursts of speed – and powerful forelegs.

The Quarter Horse may well have become defunct with the increase in popularity – due to the growing influence of the English Thoroughbred – of racing over great distances. However, his famed quarter-mile sprint was perhaps the least of his abilities.

The Quarter Horse is said to be able to 'turn on a dime and toss you back nine cents change' and it is his agility that saved him for posterity. Although he originated on the Eastern Seaboard – or east coast – of North America, when people started to spread out across the vast continent in the nineteenth century, he was used as a harness horse as well as for riding.

In the western states, his speed, agility and intelligence made him a superb ranch horse, possessing an innate 'cow

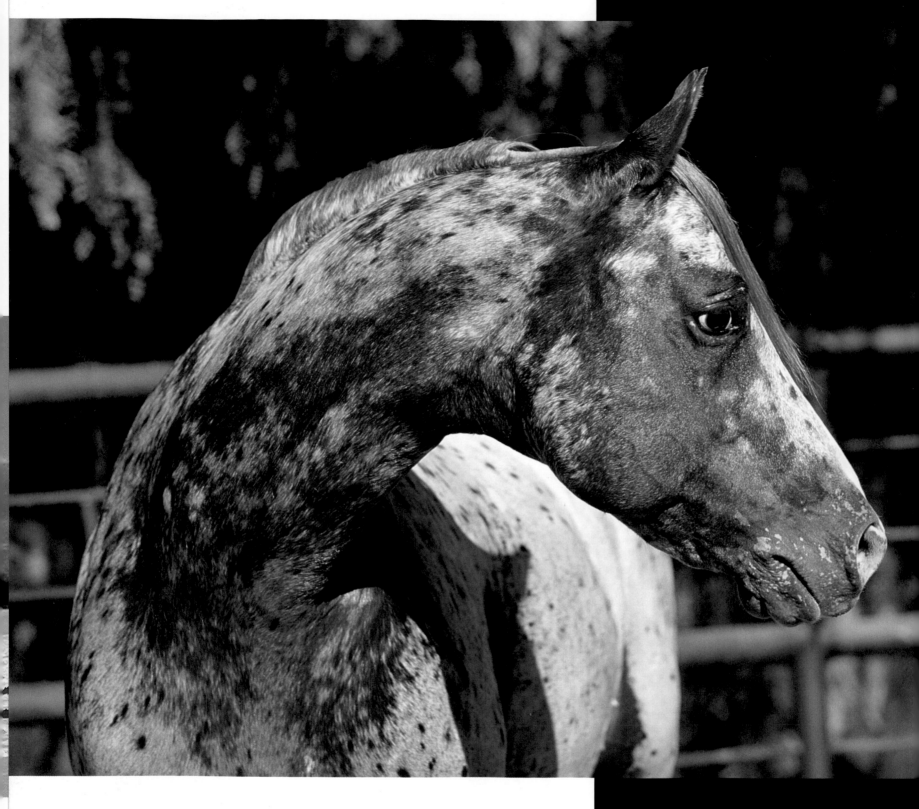

As well as his striking colouring, the Appaloosa has other distinctive characteristics. His tail is usually sparse, which the Nez Percé deemed a practical feature, because it was less likely to become entangled in thorns and shrubs.

A white *sclera* encircling the eye is a breed requirement, as is mottled skin around the muzzle. His hard, sound feet are often vertically striped.

The Nez Percé Indians and their horses were almost wiped out by the US army in 1876, but the breed was revived and is one of the most popular.

Above: *This Appaloosa shows the white sclera around the eye and the mottling of the skin on the nose and lips that is a breed characteristic*

Right: *America's National Show Horse combines the beauty of the Arabian with the charisma of the Saddlebred*

Above *A Thoroughbred mare shows off her racehorse paces*

Left: *This thoroughbred foal enjoys his early days at one of the USA's major Thoroughbred studs. The American Thoroughbred world revolves around its 'capital', Lexington, Kentucky. Here stands a statue of Man O' War, also known as Big Red, one of the most famous Thoroughbreds of the twentieth century. He was only beaten once and when he died in 1947, more than a thousand people attended his funeral*

Right: *The popularity of the Thoroughbred has increased throughout the world*

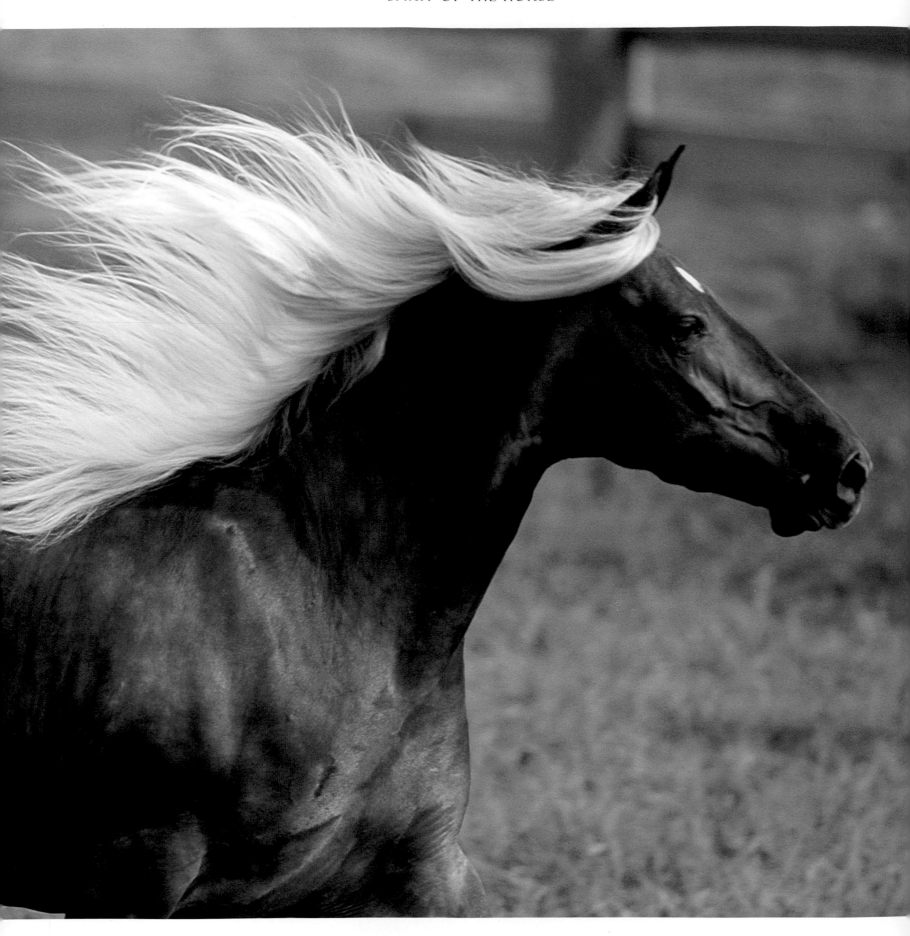

Above, right and above right: *The Rocky Mountain Pony has an unusual rich chocolate coat that does not appear in other descendants of the early Spanish imports. The full, flaxen mane and tail is a breed trait of the Rocky Mountain Pony and he is a generally good-looking, compact animal*

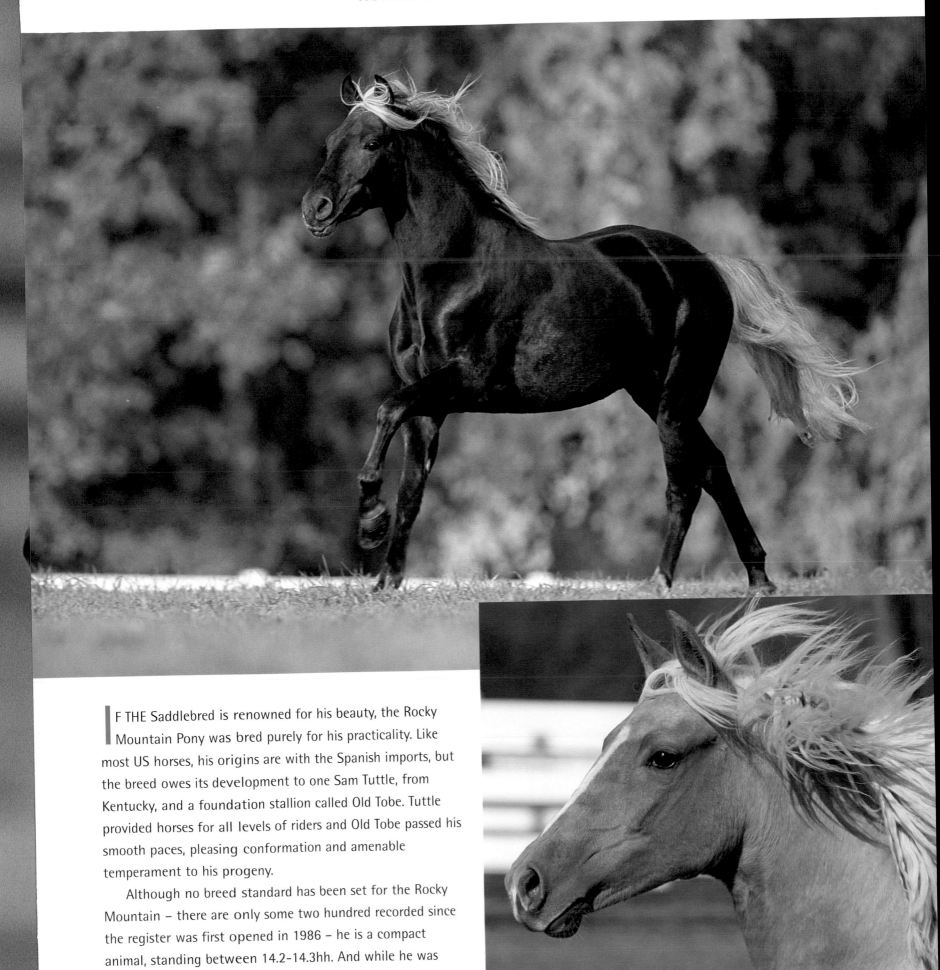

IF THE Saddlebred is renowned for his beauty, the Rocky Mountain Pony was bred purely for his practicality. Like most US horses, his origins are with the Spanish imports, but the breed owes its development to one Sam Tuttle, from Kentucky, and a foundation stallion called Old Tobe. Tuttle provided horses for all levels of riders and Old Tobe passed his smooth paces, pleasing conformation and amenable temperament to his progeny.

Although no breed standard has been set for the Rocky Mountain – there are only some two hundred recorded since the register was first opened in 1986 – he is a compact animal, standing between 14.2-14.3hh. And while he was developed as a practical, rather than ornamental, breed, he is undeniably good looking, possessing a colouring which is unusual in other equine breeds.

Above: *The Paint, or Pinto, horse only has breed status in the USA, and the Paint Horse Association divides horses into four types – stock, hunter, pleasure and saddle*

Right: *The Missouri Fox Trotter, one of the least known American breeds, was originally bred for racing, but his smooth comfortable action and ability to travel great distances at speed soon made him a popular choice for riding*

Left: *The cream or golden-coloured Palamino, another horse familiar to viewers of Western movies, and registered as a breed in the USA*

Left: *It is thought that the sire of the original Morgan was either a Thoroughbred, a Friesian or a Welsh Cob. The authority Anthony Dent maintains that 'there can be little doubt that Justin Morgan was a Welsh Cob with a touch of either Thoroughbred or Arabian'*

Below: *This handsome Morgan stallion shows the breed's fine, straight head and kind, intelligent outlook*

O F ALL the American breeds, the Morgan Horse is the oldest, and is unique in that it can be traced back to one single horse – originally called Figure, but named after his owner, Justin Morgan, on the latter's death. He was foaled in about 1790 and was acquired by his eponymous owner as a two-year-old. Although he only stood about 14hh, he was tremendously strong as well as extremely prepotent, passing on his strength, endurance and his high-stepping gait to his offspring.

His breeding is not known, although theories abound that his sire was a Thoroughbred, a Friesian or a Welsh Cob. Whatever the Morgan's original roots, he is a tough little horse with a charming nature and has been an important influence on the later American breeds.

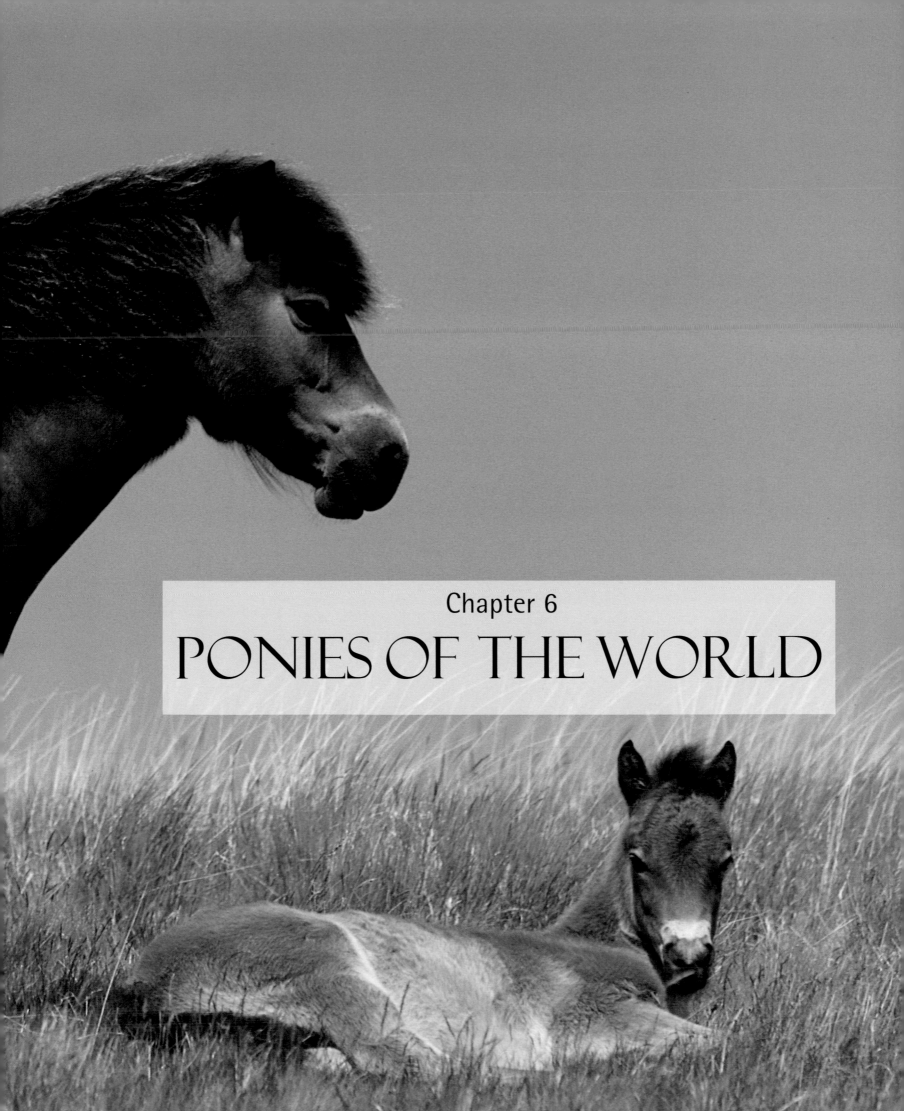

Chapter 6
PONIES OF THE WORLD

PONIES OF THE WORLD

Intelligent, crafty, cunning and kind by turn, the pony can turn on the charm to capture the hardest heart.

ANGELIC AND cheeky in equal measure, the pony, with his charm and charisma, wins the hearts of the tiniest child and the most hardened adult. Intelligent, crafty, cunning but ultimately kind, he knows exactly how to get his own way – and we invariably let him.

The world is a melting pot of pony breeds, and both the Arabian (chapter 2) and the Iberian horse (chapter 3) appear in their lineage. Great Britain, however, has some of the oldest and most prized ponies – her nine native breeds are revered worldwide and the bloodlines exported all over the world.

The Exmoor pony, for example, native to the moor of the same name on the border of North Devon and West Somerset, appears in the Domesday Book in 1085, but is thought to trace back to the Celtic ponies of the Pleistocene Age. But Spanish blood crops up in his lineage too; in 1815 a stallion, known as Katerfelto, ran on the moor. Although he was captured, it has never been determined whence he came. He was a dun horse with black points and a distinctive eel stripe. Dun ponies are occasionally seen on Exmoor today and, with bay and brown, are the only permitted colours.